A GUIDE TO

THE MILLER'S TALE

GW00708377

A GUIDE TO

THE MILLER'S TALE

PAULINE SIDEY LISOWSKA

WITH TONY BUZAN

Hodder & Stoughton

ISBN 0 340 80301 0

First published 2001
Impression number   10 9 8 7 6 5 4 3 2 1
Year   2006 2005 2004 2003 2002 2001

Cover photograph: James Tillitt 6.15 Theatre Company
Illustrations: Virginia Gray and Martin Berry
Mind Maps: Ann Jones

Typeset by Transet Limited, Coventry, England.
Printed in Great Britain for Hodder & Stoughton Educational, a division of
Hodder Headline Plc, 338 Euston Road, London NW1 3BH by Cox and Wyman Ltd,
Reading, Berks.

ONTENTS

REVISION FOR A-LEVEL LITERATURE SUCCESS

You are now in the most important educational stage of your life, and are soon to take English Literature exams that may have a major impact on your future career and goals. As one A-level student put it: 'It's crunch time!'

At this crucial stage of your life the one thing you need even more than subject knowledge is the knowledge of *how* to remember, *how* to read faster, *how* to comprehend, *how* to study, *how* to take notes and *how* to organize your thoughts. You need to know how to *think*; you need a basic introduction on how to use that super bio-computer inside your head – your brain.

The next eight pages contain a goldmine of information on how you can achieve success both at school and in your A-level English Literature exams, as well as in your professional or university career. These eight pages will give you skills that will enable you to be successful in *all* your academic pursuits. You will learn:

◆ How to recall more *while* you are learning.
◆ How to recall more *after* you have finished a class or a study period.
◆ How to use special techniques to improve your memory.
◆ How to use a revolutionary note-taking technique called Mind Maps that will double your memory and help you to write essays and answer exam questions.
◆ How to read everything faster while at the same time improving your comprehension and concentration.
◆ How to zap your revision!

How to understand, improve and master your memory of Literature Guides

Your memory really is like a muscle. Don't exercise it and it will grow weaker; *do* exercise it properly and it will grow incredibly more powerful. There are really only four main things you need to understand about your  memory in order to increase its power dramatically:

Recall during learning
– YOU MUST TAKE BREAKS!

When you are studying, your memory can concentrate, understand and recall well for between 20 and 45 minutes at a time. Then it *needs* a break. If you carry on for longer than this without one, your memory starts to break down. If you study for hours non-stop, you will remember only a fraction of what you have been trying to learn, and you will have wasted valuable revision time.

So, ideally, *study for less than an hour*, then take a five- to ten-minute break. During this break listen to music, go for a walk, do some exercise, or just daydream. (Daydreaming is a necessary brain-power booster – geniuses do it regularly.) During the break your brain will be sorting out what it has been learning and you will go back to your study with the new information safely stored and organized in your memory banks. Make *sure* you take breaks at regular intervals as you work through the *Literature Guides*.

Recall after learning
– SURFING THE WAVES OF YOUR MEMORY

What do you think begins to happen to your memory straight *after* you have finished learning something? Does it immediately start forgetting? No! Surprisingly, your brain actually *increases* its power and carries on remembering. For a short time after your study session, your brain integrates the information, making a more complete picture of everything it has just learnt. Only then does the rapid decline in memory begin, as much as 80 per cent of what you have learnt can be forgotten in a day.

However, if you catch the top of the wave of your memory, and briefly review what you have been revising at the correct time, the memory is stamped in far more strongly, and stays at the crest of the wave for a much longer time. To maximize your brain's power to remember, take a few minutes and use a Mind Map to review what you have learnt at the end of a day. Then review it at the end of a week, again at the end of a month, and finally a week before the exams. That way you'll surf-ride your memory wave all the way to your exam, success and beyond!

The memory principle of association

The muscle of your memory becomes stronger when it can **associate** – when it can link things together.

Think about your best friend, and all the things your mind *automatically* links with that person. Think about your favourite hobby, and all the associations your mind has when you think about (remember!) that hobby.

When you are studying, use this memory principle to make associations between the elements in your subjects, and thus to improve both your memory and your chances of success.

The memory principle of imagination

The muscle of your memory will improve significantly if you can produce big images in your mind. Rather than just memorizing the name of a character, imagine that character of the novel or play as if you were a video producer filming that person's life. The same goes for images in poetry.

In *all* your subjects use the **imagination** memory principle.

Throughout this *Literature Guide* you will find special association and imagination techniques (called mnemonics after the Greek goddess Mnemosyne) that will make it much easier for you to remember the topic being discussed. Look out for them!

Y*our new success formula:* *Mind Maps*®

You have noticed that when people go on holidays, or travel, they take maps. Why? To give them a general picture of where they are going, to help them locate places of special interest and importance, to help them find things more easily, and to help them remember distances and locations, etc.

It is exactly the same with your mind and with study. If you have a 'map of the territory' of what you have to learn, then everything is easier. In learning and study, the Mind Map is that special tool.

As well as helping you with all areas of study, the Mind Map actually *mirrors the way your brain works*. Your Mind Maps can be used for taking notes from your study books, for taking notes in class, for preparing your homework, for presenting your homework, for reviewing your tests, for checking your and your friends' knowledge in any subject, and for *helping you understand anything you learn*. Mind Maps are especially useful in English literature, as they allow you to map out the whole territory of a novel, play or poem, giving you an 'at-a-glance' snapshot of all the key information you need to know.

The Mind Maps in the *Literature Guide* use, throughout, **imagination** and **association**. As such, they automatically strengthen your memory muscle every time you use them. Throughout this guide you will find Mind Maps that summarize the most important areas of the English Literature guide you are studying. Study these Mind Maps, add some colour, personalize them, and then have a go at making your own Mind Maps of the work you are studying – you will remember them far better! Put them on your walls and in your files for a quick and easy review. Mind Maps are fast, efficient, effective and, importantly, *fun* to do!

HOW TO DRAW A MIND MAP

1 Start in the middle of the page with the page turned sideways. This gives your brain more radiant freedom for its thoughts.

2 Always start by drawing a picture or symbol of the novel or its title. Why? Because *a picture is worth a thousand words to your brain.* Try to use at least three colours, as colour helps your memory even more.

3 Let your thoughts flow, and write or draw your ideas on coloured branching lines connected to your central image. The key symbols and words are the headings for your topic.

4 Next, add facts and ideas by drawing more, smaller, branches on to the appropriate main branches, just like a tree.

5 Always print your word clearly on its line. Use only one word per line.

6 To link ideas and thoughts on different branches, use arrows, colours, underlining and boxes.

HOW TO READ A MIND MAP

1 Begin in the centre, the focus of your novel, play or poem.

2 The words/images attached to the centre are like chapter headings; read them next.

3 Always read out from the centre, in every direction (even on the left-hand side, where you will read from right to left, instead of the usual left to right).

USING MIND MAPS

Mind Maps are a versatile tool – use them for taking notes in class or from books, for solving problems, for brainstorming with friends, and for reviewing and revising for exams – their uses are infinite! You will find them invaluable for planning essays for coursework and exams. Number your main branches in the order in which you want to use them and off you go – the main headings for your essay are done and all your ideas are logically organized!

Super speed reading and study

What do you think happens to your comprehension as your reading speed rises? 'It goes down!' Wrong! It seems incredible, but it has been proved – the faster you read, the more you comprehend and remember!

So here are some tips to help you to practise reading faster – you'll cover the ground much more quickly, remember more, *and* have more time for revision and leisure activities!

SUPER SPEED READING

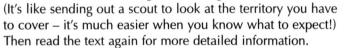

1 First read the whole text (whether it's a lengthy book or an exam paper) very quickly, to give your brain an overall idea of what's ahead and get it working. (It's like sending out a scout to look at the territory you have to cover – it's much easier when you know what to expect!) Then read the text again for more detailed information.
2 Have the text a reasonable distance away from your eyes. In this way your eye/brain system will be able to see more at a glance, and will naturally begin to read faster.
3 Take in groups of words at a time. Rather than reading 'slowly and carefully' read faster, more enthusiastically. Your comprehension will rocket!
4 Take in phrases rather than single words while you read.
5 Use a guide. Your eyes are designed to follow movement, so a thin pencil underneath the lines you are reading, moved smoothly along, will 'pull' your eyes to faster speeds.

HOW TO MAKE STUDY EASY FOR YOUR BRAIN

When you are going somewhere, is it easier to know beforehand where you are going, or not? Obviously it is easier if you *do* know. It is the same for your brain and a book. When you get a new book, there are seven things you can do to help your brain get to 'know the territory' faster:

1 Scan through the whole book in less than 20 minutes, as you would do if you were in a shop thinking whether or not to buy it. This gives your brain *control*.

2 Think about what you already know about the subject. You'll often find out it's a lot more than you thought. A good way of doing this is to do a quick Mind Map on *everything you know* after you have skimmed through it.

3 Ask who, what, why, where, when and how questions about what is in the book. Questions help your brain 'fish' the knowledge out.

4 Ask your friends what they know about the subject. This helps them review the knowledge in their own brains, and helps your brain get new knowledge about what you are studying.

5 Have another quick speed read through the book, this time looking for any diagrams, pictures and illustrations, and also at the beginnings and ends of chapters. Most information is contained in the beginnings and ends.

6 If you come across any difficult parts in your book, mark them and *move on*. Your brain *will* be able to solve the problems when you come back to them a bit later. Much like saving the difficult bits of a jigsaw puzzle for later. When you have finished the book, quickly review it one more time and then discuss it with friends. This will lodge it permanently in your memory banks.

7 Build up a Mind Map as you study the book. This helps your brain to organize and hold (remember!) information as you study.

Helpful hints for exam revision

◆ To avoid **exam panic** cram at the *start* of your course, not the end. It takes the same amount of time, so you may as well use it where it is best placed!

◆ Use Mind Maps throughout your course, and build a Master Mind Map for each subject – a giant Mind Map that summarizes everything you know about the subject.

◆ Use memory techniques such as mnemonics (verses or systems for remembering things like dates and events or lists).

◆ Get together with one or two friends to revise, compare Mind Maps, and discuss topics.

AND FINALLY ...

◆ *Have fun while you learn* – studies show that those people who enjoy what they are doing understand and remember it more, and generally do better.

◆ *Use your teachers* as resource centres. Ask them for help with specific topics and with more general advice on how you can improve your all-round performance.

◆ *Personalize your **Literature Revision Guide*** by underlining and highlighting, by adding notes and pictures. Allow your brain to have a conversation with it!

Your amazing brain and its amazing cells

Your brain is like a super, *super*, *SUPER* computer. The world's best computers have only a few thousand or hundred thousand computer chips. Your brain has 'computer chips' too, and they are called brain cells. Unlike the computer, you do not have only a few thousand computer chips – the number of brain cells in your head is a *million MILLION*!! This means you are a genius just waiting to discover yourself! All you have to do is learn how to get those brain cells working together, and you'll not only become more smart, you'll have more free time to pursue your other fun activities.

The more you understand your amazing brain the more it will repay and amaze you!

Apply its power to this *Literature Guide*!

(Tony Buzan)

OW TO USE THIS GUIDE

This guide assumes that you have already read *The Miller's Prologue and Tale*, although you could read 'Context' and 'Summaries' first. It is best to use the guide alongside the poem. You could read the 'Characterization' and 'Themes' sections without referring to the poem, but you will get more out of these if you do.

The sections

The 'Commentary' section can be used in a number of ways. One way is to read a chapter of the poem, and then read the relevant commentary. Keep on until you come to a test section, test yourself – then have a break! Alternatively, read the 'Commentary' for a section, then read that section in the poem, then go back to the 'Commentary'. See what works best for you.

'Critical approaches' sums up the main critical views and interpretations of the *The Miller's Prologue and Tale*. Your own response is important, but be aware of these approaches too.

'How to get an "A" in English Literature' gives valuable advice on what to look for in a text, and what skills you need to develop in order to achieve your personal best.

'The exam essay' is a useful 'night before' reminder of how to tackle exam questions, though it will help you more if you also look at it much earlier in the year. 'Model answer and essay plan' gives an example A-grade essay and the Mind Map and plan used to write it.

The questions

Whenever you come across a question in the guide with a star ✪ in front of it, think about it for a moment. You could make a Mini Mind Map or a few notes to focus your mind. There is not usually a 'right' answer to these: it is important for you to develop your own opinions if you want to get an 'A'. The 'Test' sections are designed to take you about 15–20 minutes each – time well spent. Take a short break after each one.

References

Line numbers refer to the Cambridge University Press edition.

KEY TO ICONS

A **theme** is an idea explored by an author. Whenever a theme is dealt with in the guide, the appropriate icon is used. This means you can find where a theme is mentioned by flicking through the book. Go on – try it now!

Secrecy and deceit

Ignorance and superstition

Pride and vanity

Love and lust

 ## STYLE AND LANGUAGE

This heading and icon are used in the Commentary wherever there is a special section on Chaucer's choice of words and imagery.

Chaucer's life

Chaucer has been described as 'the father of English poetry', and the first major English poet. Certainly he was a poet of tremendous significance, whose life experience and learning was reflected in his poetry. If you know something about the life Chaucer led and the kind of person he was, it will help to give you a greater understanding of his work.

Hint: When approaching *The Miller's Prologue and Tale*, consider the relationship between the author, the poem and the time in history it was written. This **A P T** mnemonic may help!

Author
Poem
Time

Background and upbringing

A WEALTHY FAMILY

Geoffrey Chaucer was born in London in the early 1340s, although the exact date is uncertain. His father, John Chaucer, was a wealthy wine-merchant who supplied the Royal household. The family's wealth was partly inherited from the employer of Geoffrey's grandfather, and the family changed its name to Chaucer, in honour of their deceased benefactor, having been previously known by the names of either 'Dynyngton' or 'Taverner'.

THE BENEFITS OF EDUCATION

Chaucer may well have studied at St Paul's School, London, and then gone on to study law at the Inns of Court. Chaucer's father was ambitious for his son and decided to enrol him as a page in the Royal household, serving the Countess of Ulster, the king's daughter-in-law and her husband, Prince Lionel, Duke of Clarence. This was a good way for a wealthy family not from the nobility to advance a teenage son in society. Although Chaucer was in fact a servant, or attendant, he would be able to mix with the nobility in the hope of attracting interest and patronage. Chaucer was to spend the rest of his life as a diplomat, a customs official, and Clerk of the King's Works.

FROM SOLDIER TO SPY

By his late teens Chaucer was fighting in the army of Edward III in France. He was captured and imprisoned, but was later released because the Duke paid his ransom, showing that he was of obvious importance to his master. Chaucer then began a career as a diplomat in the service of King Edward, travelling to France, Spain and Italy. It was during this time that Chaucer became familiar with European literature, especially French and Italian works. As some of his business during the next few years appears to have been kept secret, it is possible that he was in fact a spy.

MARRIAGE

When Geoffrey was in his mid-twenties he married Philippa de Roet, or Philippa Pan, a lady-in-waiting to Queen Philippa, Edward III's wife. It was a good marriage and considerably improved Geoffrey's social status. This is due to the fact that his sister-in-law Katherine later married the powerful John of Gaunt, the Duke of Lancaster and son of Edward III. The Duke was later to grant Chaucer an annual pension of ten pounds, a considerable sum in those days.

SENIOR CUSTOMS OFFICIAL

In 1374 Chaucer was appointed to the position of senior customs official which took him away from court circles but which was nevertheless of great importance. Much of the wealth of the country came from wool production, and the export market at this time was booming. Chaucer's job involved checking exports of wool. He was to remain in this post for approximately fifteen years, and during this time he no doubt came into contact with many local tradespeople who may have formed the basis for some of the characters in *The Canterbury Tales*.

MEMBER OF PARLIAMENT AND CLERK OF THE KING'S WORKS

In 1386 Geoffrey was appointed Knight of the Shire and as such could attend as a member of Parliament for Kent. Three years later King Richard II appointed him Clerk to the King's Works. This meant that he supervised all the repairs to the King's property. Unfortunately Chaucer was not successful in this position. Not only was he fairly extravagant, but he also managed to be robbed on a number of occasions, and shortly afterwards King Richard pensioned him off. Now that Chaucer was no longer in royal service he concentrated his efforts on writing his major work, *The Canterbury Tales*. When Henry IV succeeded to the throne in 1399 Chaucer was awarded a large pension of approximately 26 pounds, which meant that he could live very comfortably.

Chaucer died on 25 October 1400, with *The Canterbury Tales* unfinished. He was buried in Westminster Abbey, and his resting place is now known as 'Poets' Corner', where many major poets have since been buried.

What *are* The Canterbury Tales?

The Canterbury Tales are a collection of stories, written in verse, told by an imaginary group of pilgrims on their way to visit the shrine of Thomas à Becket at Canterbury. The work is generally thought to have been written in 1387 or 1388, and may have been partly inspired by a pilgrimage which Chaucer made around that time.

Being a man of the world, Chaucer had come into contact with people from all walks of life. Coming from a prosperous middle-class background, working in the worlds of commerce and diplomacy and yet moving in court circles would have given Chaucer a good deal of insight into the types of characters he presents us with in the *Tales.*

THE PILGRIMS

They are described as setting off from The Tabard Inn in Southwark, London, during the month of April. During the journey they tell each other stories for entertainment and as part of a story-telling competition. They are accompanied by the Host, Harry Bailly, landlord of the inn, who acts as critic and judge of their tales. The pilgrims themselves come from a wide range of backgrounds. The General Prologue mentions at least 27 pilgrims ranging from a drunken Miller and a talkative housewife from Bath, to a Knight and a Prioress from the upper echelons of society. Chaucer's pilgrims may have had characteristics easily recognizable as stereotypical to the contemporary audience, but each of them, through Chaucer's skill, is unique and three-dimensional as an individual. Each pilgrim is introduced in the General Prologue, and we discover more about them through their own, individual Prologues, through the Tales themselves, the way they are told, and also by the reactions of the other pilgrims. By using the device of pilgrims telling stories Chaucer can distance himself from what is being said, so that the Miller's crudeness, for example, can be dismissed as in keeping with the character created rather than the author. In this way Chaucer the poet is made to disappear, and is eventually booed off!

THE STORIES

The stories themselves have many and various subjects and themes. Some of them, like so many stories in the Middle Ages, are told partly for entertainment and partly to instruct the audience. *The Nun's Priest's Tale*, for example, takes the form of a moral fable using animals with human characteristics to make observations about human nature – rather as George Orwell later did in *Animal Farm*. Other tales, such as *The Knight's Tale*, follow the courtly love tradition. These courtly romances concerned love affairs amongst the nobility where a woman was placed on a pedestal and idolized from afar. Her admirer would try to win her favour by attempting to complete nearly impossible tasks. In contrast to these elegant romances some of the other Tales take the form of bawdy romps and sexually explicit farces such as *The Miller's Tale* and *The Reeve's Tale*.

PILGRIMAGES IN CHAUCER'S TIME

By the fourteenth century it was common practice for people to make journeys to places of special religious significance, for example, a saint's shrine. Such journeys were usually undertaken for the purpose of religious devotion, to offer thanks, or to atone for sins. Pilgrims normally travelled together to provide each other with company and for reasons of safety. Traditionally, pilgrims would be dressed simply, and could be recognized by the emblem of a cockle shell worn on their hats, and by the staffs that they carried. Pilgrimages could last for many days, weeks or months, and pilgrims would visit sacred places in continental Europe, such as Compostela in Spain, Cologne in Germany, or even travel as far afield as the Holy Land.

In England one of the most popular places to visit was the shrine of St Thomas à Becket at Canterbury in Kent. Thomas was Chancellor of England and Archbishop of Canterbury in the twelfth century. After a quarrel with King Henry II he was murdered by some of Henry's nobles in 1170. He was canonized as a saint and a martyr in 1173, and miracles were said to have occurred at his tomb.

By the time that Chaucer's pilgrims were gathering to make the journey to Canterbury, pilgrimages were undertaken not just for devotional reasons. The journeys themselves became seen as being opportunities for business enterprise or as a popular pastime. Pilgrimages were seen as part of a growing tourist industry with hotels being set up along pilgrimage routes or by sacred sites. Businesses that provided travellers with horses or that offered sea transport were established, and travel guides were produced. In addition, relics and religious souvenirs which pilgrims could purchase also became business opportunities for entrepreneurs at the religious places themselves.

As you can imagine, these led to marvellous opportunities for fraud and forgery, with numerous relics of 'the True Cross' being sold, or threads 'from the handkerchief used to wipe the face of Christ on the road to Calvary' being offered as authentic to unsuspecting pilgrims. Any relics which were brought back from pilgrimages were considered as being enormously important and precious. At Canterbury it was possible to buy all sorts of badges, holy water phials and other souvenirs quite legitimately, as Rome had given the monasteries permission to manufacture them for sale.

In *The Canterbury Tales* Chaucer satirizes the false claims to the authenticity of holy relics in his description of the Pardoner, who is definitely a fraudster! The Wife of Bath, who seems to be almost a professional pilgrim, may well have been using her trips for business or tourist reasons, rather than for devotional purposes. The Miller, who has appointed himself usher to the rest of the company, seems to have more interest in drink and wrestling than religion. On the other hand, the Knight is a serious and devout man who has been abroad fighting for the Christian cause and still has the marks of his armour stained into his tunic.

WHY CHOOSE A PILGRIMAGE AS A BASIS FOR A POEM?

Imagine a group of people from varied backgrounds and from different walks of life. They each have a story to tell. Some of the stories may be funny, some sad. Some stories may have a moral to them. Also, the people in the group may not get on with each other, and so might try to score points off each other. You then send them off on a journey together. What might happen? The dramatic possibilities are endless, and so are the opportunities for the writer, both for satire (holding up follies and vices to ridicule) and seriousness. This is what *The Canterbury Tales* is all about. In the hands of such a talented artist as Chaucer, the device of the pilgrimage is highly original and successful.

What else did Chaucer write?

Chaucer was an extremely well-read man. He owned approximately sixty books, which is a huge number by fourteenth-century standards. His own works, including *The Canterbury Tales*, show the influence of classical, biblical and contemporary writings.

Chaucer's first major work, the *Roman de la Rose*, was a translation of a French romance, a tale of chivalry, originally written in verse, and deals with all aspects of love. The work also contains much satirical material at the expense of women. His second important work was most likely *The Book of the Duchess*, written in the 1370s as a tribute to Blanche, the deceased wife of John of Gaunt. This was followed by *The*

Parlement of Fowles (c.1380–82) which tells of how the birds (the 'fowls' of the title) choose their mates on St Valentine's Day and of the difficulties the eagle has in choosing her mate from among several suitors. This work may have been written for the marriage of Richard II to Anne of Bohemia, who had many previous offers of marriage before making her choice.

Chaucer's great dramatic poem, *Troilus and Criseyde* (c.1385) set against the background of the Trojan Wars, deals with the ill-fated love affair between Prince Troilus and the beautiful Criseyde, who later betrays him in favour of Diomede, a Greek commander.

Since Chaucer had criticized women in both the *Roman de la Rose* and *Troilus and Criseyde*, he set out to redress the balance in his poem *The Legend of Good Women*. In this poem, Chaucer promises Cupid, the god of love, to tell only good stories about women in the future.

Historical and social background

Chaucer's extensive knowledge of scholarly and ecclesiastical writings, as well as contemporary beliefs and opinions, is shown throughout *The Canterbury Tales*. For example, *The Miller's Tale* shows us a variety of contemporary attitudes towards religion, astrology, and sexual relationships. You will find that modern society's opinions on these topics are very different from those of the fourteenth century. When you are studying the text, try to avoid judging the ideas and characters by modern standards. Instead, look for the ways in which the text reflects, challenges, or satirizes the established order of its day.

Words and concepts

The Miller's Prologue and Tale will introduce you to some important concepts with which you may not be familiar, being specific to the period of time in which it was written. These ideas are crucial to your understanding of the text.

REEVE

In feudal law the manorial courts, which had jurisdiction over tenants, were overseen by a steward or Reeve. The Reeve of *The Canterbury Tales* was also a craftsman, a carpenter by trade.

HENDE

On eleven occasions throughout the Tale, Nicholas is referred to as *hende Nicholas.* This word has several meanings and Chaucer uses it to good effect, making the most of its ambiguous nature. *Hende* had been used to mean 'gentle', 'courteous' and 'gracious' in the courtly romances, but Chaucer uses it to describe Nicholas in an ironic way, meaning 'slick', 'handy', or 'on-the-spot', to suggest Nicholas's opportunistic and far from courteous nature!

COURTLY LOVE (FINE AMOUR)

The courtly love tradition, as it is known, partly grew out of the medieval worship of the purity, beauty and innocence of the Virgin Mary (see 'The Status of women', p. 19). Courtly love involved only those people from the nobility, and concerned a love triangle between a married woman and her lover. It was a very formal affair with strict rules. Basically the lovesick suitor would worship and admire the woman from afar. He would go to extreme lengths to win her favour, dedicating his achievements to her while he suffered in silence, waiting for her to take notice of him. When she eventually did so, the lover was elevated by the experience and ennobled by it. There are many examples in literature of the period of this love ritual, for example, Chaucer's translation of *The Romance of the Rose* and *The Knight's Tale* (see 'Literary background', p. 20).

GENTILLESSE

At the end of the Miller's Prologue Chaucer anticipates that the themes of certain other Tales would touch upon the qualities of *gentillesse,/ And eek moralitee and hoolinesse.* Whereas *moralitee* and *hoolinesse* could be said to have meanings loosely equivalent to their modern counterparts, *gentillesse* as a concept may not be quite so familiar, and has no real modern-day equivalent. Basically *gentillesse* linked virtue with high birth. It was thought that persons of the nobility automatically inherited the virtues of chivalry, courtesy, generosity and morality. In other words these people were considered to be *gentil* in their behaviour.

ASTROLOGIE, ASTRONOMYE

Astrology is the scientific study of heavenly bodies as in astronomy, except that it also concerns the influence of the stars and planets on the earth and human destiny. It was considered to be an extremely important and serious field of study in the fourteenth century, and Chaucer himself practised it. The average person – such as a carpenter – would have little scientific knowledge, but would not question the concept of planetary influence.

As can be seen in *The Miller's Tale* the study of astronomy and astrology was tied up considerably with religion. Thomas Aquinas, one of the leading theologians of the medieval period, considered that if the moon could influence the tides then there was no reason why the stars and planets could not influence human affairs. He did not, however, believe that astrology should be used for predicting the future. This is because the Church considered that the heavenly bodies were associated with the creative power of God, and astrological prediction would involve a kind of celestial 'spying' on the Almighty.

The student Nicholas is passionate about astrology and astronomy. His room contains a treasured copy of the classical Greek scholar Ptolemy's treatise on astronomy, the *Almageste*. In addition he owns scientific equipment to help him perform the complex mathematical calculations necessary for his study, such as an astrolabe and augrim stones. Chaucer wrote about the use of an astrolabe in his *Treatise on the Astrolabe* which he dedicated to his son Lewis. It would have been easy for an uneducated man such as John to be duped by Nicholas, and fearful that an over-zealous study of the heavens might bring about divine retribution.

DREAMS AND SUPERSTITIONS

Many people in the fourteenth century were superstitious, and superstitions were taken seriously. In *The Miller's Tale*, both John the carpenter and Absolon the parish clerk show themselves to be superstitious. Dreams were also taken seriously as portents of future events. Several other of *The Canterbury Tales*, including the Wife of Bath's and the Nun's Priest's, show the influence of dreams. For example, Absolon dreams of a feast which he takes to indicate future sexual fulfilment with Alison. It proves not to be a feast to Absolon's taste! Here Chaucer uses dreamlore for the purposes of irony.

Hint: Look out for how Chaucer presents and uses these concepts and words in *The Miller's Tale*. He may be using them in a satirical way, or to make a moral point.

The social structure

The social structure in the fourteenth century was much more rigid than it is today. People's opinions and beliefs, and their position in society, were part of an established order. This order was hierarchical, and men were placed higher in status than women. The king, who was appointed by God, was highest in rank. After the king came the nobility – Dukes and Earls who were either related to the king or interrelated amongst themselves. Next came the gentility, the knights and burgesses who held low-level judicial and political positions. The rest consisted of everybody below the gentry and in hierarchical rank according to land and wealth. Below the gentry came the yeomen – men who owned sixty or more acres of land; below them were the husbandman who helped run the larger farms. At the bottom of the social scale were the labourers, servants, peasants and serfs.

In the Prologue to *The Miller's Tale* Chaucer refers to the Miller and Reeve as being *cherls*, which in theory could mean any of the lower echelons of society. However, Chaucer is using this word to imply that these characters are base, and have base manners. At the beginning of the Tale the carpenter is pinpointed as being of the yeoman class, being master of his trade and having a good income. He adds to his wealth by taking in lodgers. However, he is also referred to as a *gnof*, or

KNIGHT

PARSON

FRIAR

PRIORESS

REEVE

COOK

WIFE OF BATH

CLERK

lout, because of his low education and ignorance. It is interesting to note that although Nicholas is far better educated than John, he has to defer to the carpenter as his senior and his landlord. Nicholas certainly rejects this deferential position and is scathing about the carpenter's ignorance compared with his own intellectual superiority. Alison, the carpenter's wife, is described by the Miller as being attractive enough to make her the mistress of any lord, but is only fit to be the wife of a yeoman. In other words a nobleman might sleep with her, but would consider Alison far too low in social status to contemplate marrying her. Chaucer's pilgrims are introduced roughly in order of their rank, with the Knight, who comes from the nobility, leading the order. The Wife of Bath, who comes from the middle classes, is introduced approximately halfway through the list of pilgrims, and the lowly Miller and Ploughman near the end.

THE FEUDAL SYSTEM

Society was still based on the feudal system in the fourteenth century. That is, the land was owned by wealthy lords, and the peasants who worked the land were more or less owned by their master, to whom they were bound by duty and loyalty.

THE BLACK DEATH

The fourteenth century was also a period of change, and saw many challenges to the established order. One of the most devastating occurrences which contributed to the social, economic and political changes was the Plague, or 'Black Death'.

Chaucer was still a child when the bubonic plague, which had ravaged Europe since 1347, arrived in England in 1349. The disease wiped out approximately a third of the population. No one knew that 'the Death' was spread by rat fleas. Considering the huge numbers of rats and the standards of fourteenth-century hygiene, conditions were rife for an epidemic, and the plague rapidly swept through the country. More and more people succumbed, their bodies becoming swollen and blackened. It is difficult to imagine the fear and superstition which must have spread at this time, and the powerful effect it must have had on all aspects of society in the Middle Ages. No wonder the carpenter is fearful when he thinks that his lodger

Nicholas might be ill, and contemplates the recent, swift death of an apparently fit person!

> *This world is now ful tikel, sikerly.*
> *I saugh to-day a cors yborn to chirche*
> *That now, on Monday last, I saugh him wirche.*

SOCIAL MOBILITY AND THE PEASANTS' REVOLT

As 'the Death' had killed off much of the peasant population there were fewer people available to labour on the old estates. Those people who had survived the plague often inherited the property and wealth of their less fortunate relatives. This created a new social class of wealthy town-dwellers: merchants, physicians, cooks and business people – including Chaucer's own family, who rose from being inn-keepers to moving in court circles in three generations (see 'Chaucer's life', pp. 1–3).

The events of the fourteenth century may have offered opportunities to move out of the social class into which one was born, but not everyone was happy with this upward mobility. Many of those who had previously held power felt threatened, and various steps were taken to curb any further changes to the social order. Laws were passed to make it illegal for peasants to seek higher wages or work for different masters. A poll tax of one shilling was imposed on every adult in the country, irrespective of whether they were rich or poor. For many, this unfair tax was the last straw and people became bitter and discontented. In 1381 this led to outright rebellion and the Peasants' Revolt, led by Wat Tyler. Violence broke out in the south-east and spread to London . This would almost certainly have affected Chaucer, who lived close to the centre of the civil unrest.

The Peasants' Revolt was the result of huge social and economic injustice, and the wealthy landlords found themselves the targets of the uprising. The Church itself was, in fact, a wealthy landlord, and the large, rich monasteries of the south-east found themselves under attack. These attacks culminated in the execution of the Archbishop of Canterbury himself by the rebel leader, Wat Tyler. In order to understand the causes of this hatred we have to know something about the position of the Church in England in the fourteenth century.

The Church

POWER

The Church had a huge and powerful influence on virtually every aspect of fourteenth-century life. Everyone was expected to attend Masses, go to confession and contribute to church funds. Churches contained many beautiful paintings, carvings and stonework. The Masses and religious ceremonies were musical and theatrical. This meant that the Church provided the main, and possibly the only, artistic experience that an ordinary person was likely to get in everyday life. The Church had real political and economic power, but, like many institutions which become particularly powerful, it was open to corruption. The clergy held important offices in government, including that of treasurer of the realm, which led to criticism of the Church holding the purse-strings of the country.

WEALTH

The Church had in fact become hugely wealthy. Monasteries owned vast estates and employed large numbers of peasants to farm the land. In large cathedral towns, such as Canterbury, everyone who lived on the estates came under the rule of the Church in secular, as well as spiritual matters. The workers would be paid by the Church who would own the houses and food which the estate produced. As additional sources of revenue, monasteries would offer hospitality at a price to wealthy travellers. Chaucer's pilgrims, for example, would have each paid a groat (approximately twice the average daily wage for a labourer) to sleep on straw mattresses at Canterbury cathedral. In some instances the monasteries also provided what were, in fact, the only proper hospitals and schools for the community. In *The Miller's Tale* the monastery at Osney and the church in Oxford both play a significant part in the community. For instance, the carpenter appears to pay regular visits to the monastery in Osney to get supplies of timber, and Absolon, the parish clerk, is described as being a good barber and blood-letter. The Church therefore had huge influence in many areas of people's lives.

EDUCATION

There was little in the way of formal education, and certainly not for girls, as the monasteries ran the small number of grammar schools in existence, and girls were not welcome. The grammar schools offered education to clever boys from poor families. These boys would then go on to become clerks attached to the monastery or could be sent to study at the universities of Oxford or Cambridge. Nicholas is a student at Oxford, and is apparently helped to remain there by donations from his friends as well as using his own funds. In addition to his ecclesiastical studies Nicholas would study a variety of other subjects including astrology, astronomy, grammar, logic and rhetoric. Absolon is described as *the parisshe clerk*. He works for the church in various ways, acting as barber and blood-letter, drawing up legal agreements and swinging the censer during the Masses.

LAW

If a member of the clergy had committed an offence he could be tried only in an ecclesiastical court, which would be able to show considerable bias! In addition, all members of the clergy had the right to appeal to the Pope.

PAPACY

The papacy was not without its problems. In the early part of the fourteenth century, the papacy had moved from Rome to Avignon in France, only to find its power challenged by the setting up of a rival pope in Rome. This understandably caused confusion over who the real head of the Church was!

CORRUPTION AND CRITICISM

In England there was growing criticism of the power and wealth of the Church. This criticism came from many quarters of society. In Parliament, the Commons argued that the Church had power over the country's revenue as the treasury was in ecclesiastical hands. In towns and cities such as London the new middle class became open in their criticism. In addition, discontent was growing within the Church. Poor priests, angry at the wealth of the bishops and abbots, went about the country preaching the virtues of humility and self-control, and mocking the excesses of the rich. Chaucer's poor Parson in the *Tales* is one of these priests. Members of the clergy were regularly satirized in literature for being greedy, corrupt and hypocritical.

The monarchy

In 1377 the young King Richard II came to the English throne, aged only ten. It was a particularly difficult time for the monarchy. The England that Richard inherited had been ravaged by plague and was beset with heavy taxes due to the costly 'Hundred Years War' (1337–80) with France. The young king also had to cope with attacks from Parliament which were fought off successfully with the help of his uncle, John of Gaunt, the Duke of Lancaster. When Richard was just 14 he managed to cope with another destabilizing influence – the Peasants' Revolt of 1381, quashing the rebellion with his courage and daring. Richard was also threatened by challenges from some of his own nobles. On his return from an expedition to Ireland in 1399, he discovered that Henry Bolingbroke had mustered a large army against him. Richard was eventually defeated in Wales, and imprisoned in Pontefract Castle, where he died in February 1400.

CHRONOLOGY OF CHAUCER'S LIFE AND TIMES

1340–5	Chaucer born.
1346	English victory at Crecy.
1348–50	Plague.
1349–51	Boccaccio's *Decameron* (with account of Plague); 1350 Renaissance begins in Italy.
1356	English victory at Poitiers.
1357	Chaucer a page in the household of the Countess of Ulster.
1359–60	Chaucer serves in war in France. Captured by French; ransomed for £16.
1361–2	Severe recurrence of Plague.
1360s	Langland's *Piers Plowman*.

1366	Chaucer marries Phillippa de Roet and travels to Spain.
1367	Birth of Chaucer's son, Thomas. Chaucer a squire in court of Edward III.
1368	Chaucer travels to the Continent (possibly France) on 'the King's service'.
1368–72	Chaucer writes *Roman de la Rose* (*Romance of the Rose*) and *The Book of the Duchess*.
1369	Chaucer serves in John of Gaunt's army in France.
1372	Chaucer travels to Italy on a diplomatic mission.
1374	Death of Petrarch. Chaucer granted a gallon of wine daily for life. Controller of Customs.
1375	Death of Boccaccio.
1376–7	Several trips to France, negotiating for peace and marriage of Richard.
1377	Edward III dies; Richard II crowned.
1380	*Raptus* of Cecilia Chaumpaigne.
1380	Birth of Chaucer's second son, Lewis.
1380	Chaucer writes *The Parlement of Fowles*.
1381	Peasant's Revolt.
1382	Chaucer writes *Troilus and Criseyde*.
1385–7	Chaucer writes *The Legend of Good Women*.
1386	Chaucer serves as MP for Kent.
1387–92	*Canterbury Tales* begun.
1389	Chaucer appointed Clerk to the King's Works.
1390	Chaucer robbed of horse, goods and £20 in Surrey.
c.1396	Chaucer writes *The Envoy to Buckton*, urging the addressee to read *The Wife of Bath*.
1396– 1400	Chaucer writes latest of Tales, including possibly *The Nun's Priest's Tale*.
1398	Chaucer is granted a tun of wine a year.
1399	Richard deposed; Henry IV crowned.
1400	Chaucer dies (25 October, according to tradition).

The status of women

MALE DOMINANCE

Medieval society was dominated by men; women had virtually no political, legal or economic power in their own right. They were considered to be little more than property; even rape was seen as a property crime. Any wealth that they had would pass automatically to their husbands on marriage, who would assume authority over them.

ANTI-FEMINISM: EVE

Women were seen very much as of secondary importance in medieval society. They were thought to be inferior in intellect and power to men, and to symbolize the flesh, while men symbolized reason. This view had its source in biblical and ecclesiastical writings and was perpetuated by the teachings of the Church which stated that women were the root of all humanity's sufferings. This is because of what happened in the Garden of Eden, according to the Book of Genesis, when Eve's weakness led to Adam's downfall and their subsequent expulsion from Eden.

ADORATION: THE VIRGIN MARY

The polar opposite to this was the medieval 'worship' of the Virgin Mary, who, as the mother of Christ, symbolized all that was pure, holy and fine in womankind: beautiful and yet an untouched virgin – and a loving mother. The elevation of woman in the courtly love tradition had its origins in this adoration of Mary. The attitude of the Church towards women was therefore ambiguous. On the one hand there was Eve, reviled by ecclesiastical teachings, but on the other hand the Virgin Mary (a descendant of Eve) commanded the Church's adoration.

MARRIAGE

Marriages did not happen for love. Rather, they took place on purely economic grounds. There were even cases of young daughters actually being sold by parents to 'suitable' partners. It was also not uncommon for a young daughter to be married off to someone many years her senior, if it meant a good economic and social match. The beautiful 18-year-old Alison, described as fit *For any lord to leggen in his bedde,/ Or yet for any good yeman to wedde*, is married to John, the carpenter, a man much older than herself. The Miller himself is disapproving of this mismatched pair, and the subsequent events in the Tale leading up to the gulling of the carpenter certainly show that the situation of youth marrying age is far from ideal. Moreover the supposition was that wives, being the 'weaker' sex, would be unfaithful, as the Miller's Prologue suggests.

Literary background

THE OLD TESTAMENT: NOAH'S FLOOD

According to the Old Testament of the Bible, God saw all the wickedness in the world and decided to destroy it and start again. God determined to send a great Flood to wipe out all life. However, Noah, an upright man, and his family were to be preserved. God told Noah to build an ark which he and his family could board to save them from drowning. After the waters subsided, God sent a rainbow as a promise never to send another Flood to destroy the earth. Nicholas uses John's inadequate knowledge of this Bible story to dupe him.

MYSTERY PLAYS

This was a popular form of theatre during the Middle Ages. The themes of the plays were religious, dealing with biblical subjects such as the Creation, the Fall of Man, or the Nativity, but the spirit of the plays was essentially secular. It was common for the storylines to depart from the Bible completely, and for monsters and demons to be introduced into the drama. The plays were performed in the vernacular as opposed to Latin, and this increased their popularity with the audience.

During the thirteenth and fourteenth centuries, the plays were staged by guilds of tradesmen, and they were organized into cycles according to their subject matter. It was common for large towns, such as York or Chester, to have their own cycle of plays, and for the guild who had some obvious association with the subject matter of the drama to perform a particular part of the cycle. For instance, the building of Noah's ark would be performed by the shipwrights. The plays were staged using mobile carts or pageant wagons, often with high scaffolding as part of the stage area. They were one of the only forms of real entertainment for the fourteenth-century audience, and provided a certain amount of religious instruction, albeit somewhat sketchy! Very few people in the fourteenth century could read or write, books were few and far between, there was no universal education, and the Latin masses could not always be fully understood.

A complete Mystery cycle, starting with the Creation, and ending with the Last Judgement, provided a staged version of the history of the world. However, exact history as told by the Bible, was sometimes overwhelmed by the need to present exciting theatre. The carpenter shows himself to have a limited idea of the story of Noah; if he had known the biblical version better he would have remembered that God promised Noah that there would never be another Flood. In addition, he would know that all the fuss about Mrs Noah refusing to board the ark was just a piece of comic entertainment devised for the Mystery Plays. As it is, John's limited and inaccurate biblical knowledge makes him an easy target for the wily Nicholas. In addition to the story of the Flood, the medieval audience may well have been familiar with the Mystery Play which tells of Joseph's shame at Mary's pregnancy, and his belief that marrying a much younger woman can only cause trouble. Joseph, like John in *The Miller's Tale*, is also a carpenter! This sequence can be seen today in the York Mystery cycle.

THE POPULAR STORY

The medieval audience expected the retelling of a popular story or folktale. Creating an original plot was less important than the way in which the story was told, and this was the job of the poet. In fact, if a new story was created, it was not unusual to pretend that it was simply a new slant on an old tale.

ROMANCES AND COURTLY LOVE

The upper class convention of courtly, or chivalric, love first expressed itself in the troubadour poetry of southern France in the eleventh century. The essence of the convention was shown in these literary romances: the courtly lover existed to serve his lady and he formed part of an adulterous love triangle in an age where marriages were based on business or power alliances. The Roman poet Ovid in his *Ars amatoria* would also have influenced this genre in that he pictured the lover as a slave of passion, sighing and even dying for his love. The courtly lover was filled with respect and adoration for the object of his affection.

In the twelfth century, Eleanor of Aquitaine inspired some of the best troubadour poetry. Her daughter, Marie of Champagne, encouraged the poet Chrétien de Troyes to write *Launcelot*, a courtly romance whose hero obeys every request (reasonable and unreasonable) of the heroine. The works of great poets such as Dante and Petrarch, contemporaries of Chaucer, also contain examples of this love ritual, Petrarch writing sonnets to 'Laura', and Dante immortalizing 'Beatrice' in his great work *La divina commedia.* Chaucer himself translated *The Romance of the Rose*, and *The Knight's Tale* also represents the genre of courtly love, where two lovers, Arcite and Palamon, are rivals for the same girl, worshipping her from afar.

FABLIAUX

A 'fabliau' (plural 'fabliaux') can be defined as a short metrical tale made popular in France in the thirteenth and early fourteenth centuries by professional storytellers. Fabliaux were characterized by vivid, realistic detail and an erotic plot line which was usually comic, coarse, irreverent and cynical, especially where women were concerned. The situations of the characters in the stories and their adventures were often obscene. Stock characters kept appearing in fabliaux, such as the cuckold, his wife, and the naughty priest. Often the plot showed the deceiver being deceived, and the plots, although convincing, required degrees of gullibility on the part of their victims.

Unlike the romances of courtly love, which involved the nobility, fabliaux presented lively images of life among the middle and lower classes. The practical jokes, gullings and cuckoldings do not always coincide with conventional morality, but have their own kind of 'justice' within the tales. Pride and greed are often punished, but so are jealous husbands – especially old ones. The heroes and heroines are nearly always young and witty. The victims are those whom society usually respects, such as prosperous merchants or hardworking tradesmen. The genre is therefore delightfully subversive.

This form of literature was not just popular with the ordinary people, but it also appealed to the upper classes, especially if the fabliau included an element of parody, such as parody of the courtly love genre, which would require a good knowledge of courtly love, language and manners for its full comic effect. This would mean that the upper echelons of society may well enjoy themselves laughing at those humble folk in the stories who try to imitate their betters! *The Miller's Tale*, *The Reeve's Tale*, *The Shipman's Tale*, and *The Summoner's Tale* are all examples of fabliaux.

FABLIAUX SIMILAR TO THE MILLER'S TALE

There are several examples of contemporary fabliaux which are similar in plot to *The Miller's Tale*. One such example is the early thirteenth-century French fabliau *Bèrenger of the Long Arse*, which shows the humiliation of a churlish, proud and cowardly husband, who is made to kiss the backside of his wife, who has disguised herself as a fearsome knight called 'Sir Bèrenger'.

The fourteenth-century Flemish story *Heile of Bersele* tells a story similar to *The Miller's Tale*. Its heroine is a courtesan who is desired by three men, a smith, a priest and a miller, each of whom visit her at different times of night (corresponding to curfew, cock crow and lauds of *The Miller's Tale*). However, on one occasion the clients arrive at the same time. The miller hides in a trough which hangs from the ceiling, the priest is allowed into the house and starts to enjoy himself but on hearing the smith outside begging for a kiss, puts his rear end out of the bedroom window and is burned by the smith's red-hot poker.

Other similar fabliaux are *The Smith in the Kneading Tub*, *Viola and her lovers* and *Old Hogyn's Adventure*, which all show foolish old husbands being cuckolded, misplaced kisses, and brandings on the rump, very like *The Miller's Tale*.

FACT FILE

The difference between fabliau and romance can briefly be said to be that the romance explores the possibility that men can behave nobly and unselfishly, whereas the fabliau shows people behaving in a degraded way. In other words:

- *Romance*: **R**uling class courting madly
- *Fabliau*: **F**olk behaving badly

CHAUCER

The Prologue

The Knight finishes his story and the whole company thinks he has told a noble tale. The drunken Miller claims that he has a tale which is just as noble as the Knight's and he demands to tell it next. The Host tries to intervene but the Miller becomes aggressive and threatening, so reluctantly the Host lets him have his way. The Miller says that his tale will be about a carpenter and his wife and will show how the carpenter is cuckolded by his lodger, a student. The carpenter (the Reeve) objects but the Miller carries on regardless. The narrator apologizes for the forthcoming Tale, admitting that the Miller is not well-bred and will therefore tell a bawdy story.

The Tale

John, a rich old carpenter, lives in Oxford with his wife, the pretty 18-year-old Alison, of whom he is jealously fond. He has a lodger called Nicholas, a student at the university who is attracted to Alison and wants to sleep with her. She agrees to become his lover and Nicholas thinks up a plan to get John out of the way so they can spend the night together. Also living in Oxford is the parish clerk, an effeminate dandy called Absolon. He also desires Alison and tries to woo her, but he is too late as Nicholas is there first.

Nicholas has a passion for astrology, and he tricks the credulous John into believing a prediction that there is going to be a second Flood, which only himself, John and Alison will survive. John makes three tubs, which he ties to the roof beam in which they can float until the floodwaters subside. On the day the supposed Flood is due, they all climb into their tubs. When John is asleep, Alison and Nicholas tiptoe down to the bedroom and jump into bed together. They are interrupted by Absolon outside the window who has come to woo Alison.

Alison promises him a kiss, but for a joke sticks her backside out of the window and Absolon kisses it by mistake.

As soon as Absolon has realized his mistake he wants revenge. He goes and gets a red-hot plough blade from the local blacksmith and returns to the window. Absolon says that if Alison gives him another kiss he will give her a gold ring. This time Nicholas puts his backside out of the window, and Absolon burns it with the hot coulter. Nicholas yells out in pain. The carpenter wakes up, thinks the Flood has come, and cuts the rope tying his tub to the ceiling. He falls to the ground, knocking himself unconscious and breaking his arm. The neighbours rush to the scene to see what is going on and are convinced that old John is mad.

Try this

? The following pictures represent some of the major influences present in fourteenth-century England. Add your own keywords to each.

Take a short break before you meet the Miller, and the famous four from Oxford.

C HARACTERIZATION

The Miller

We learn from the General Prologue, and the Prologue to *The Miller's Tale,* that Robin the Miller is a big bruiser of a man and a prize wrestler. He is so strong that he can heave a door off its hinges or ram it with his head. He is decidedly unpleasant to look at. He has a red beard as broad as a spade, and a wart on his nose from which red bristles spring. His nostrils are black and wide, and his mouth is as large as a furnace door. He carries a sword and buckler by his side and a set of bagpipes to play the company of pilgrims out of London. He has an unpleasant personality to match his appearance. He is a joker who has a store of dirty stories which he delights in telling when he visits taverns. He is also a cheat who steals corn and still expects to be well paid! He is over-fond of his beer and becomes argumentative and threatening when told that he ought not to tell his story after the well-bred Knight's noble tale. Chaucer describes him as a *cherl.*

MILLER

John

John is an elderly, rich, successful carpenter who is adept at his trade and makes a good living in Oxford and the surrounding area. He has recently married a much younger woman, Alison, of whom he is jealous and suspicious. The fact that he is just newly married and could hardly fail to realize Alison's sex appeal, no doubt makes him twice as possessive as he already is. In spite of these fears, John is apparently fond of her and indulges her in nice clothes and jewellery. John's character is defined almost entirely by his attitude to Alison. He may well truly show concern for her, but keeping her *narwe in cage* shows the limitations of his possessive type of love.

One of Chaucer's most characteristic traits of style is the ability to define character in terms of physical appearance. This is not the case with John. Instead we are only told that he is 'old';

the stereotype of an elderly, jealous man, someone the audience may well see as deserving his fate. At least the Miller mentions honestly that Alison was a handful and John would just need to put up with it, if he was foolish enough to marry someone so much younger in the first place.

We discover that John is uneducated, foolish, credulous and pious, although his piety is linked with superstition. He supplements his wealth by taking in lodgers, such as the clever student Nicholas. John views Nicholas's studies with a mixture of respect and scorn. His superstitious nature makes him an easy target for Nicholas's wiles, for he definitely believes that Nicholas might bring divine retribution on his house through his passion for astrology, and so sets about exorcizing his property with a 'night-spell' to ward off demons. John's uneducated and gullible nature makes him believe Nicholas's ruse about the second Flood, and he works on the ridiculous task of creating boats from tubs, stringing them up from the ceiling. John eventually ends up a cuckold with a broken arm, and is thought of as mad.

Alison

Alison's character is by far the most two-dimensional of the four major characters in the Tale; whereas the other male characters develop, Alison remains exactly the same from start to finish.

Alison is the 18-year-old wife of the elderly carpenter. She is an attractive and lively girl who is very aware of the constraints of her position as John's wife. She tells Nicholas *Myn housbonde is so ful of jalousie/ That but ye waite wel and been privee,/ I woot right wel I nam but deed.* She is extremely proud of her appearance, taking care that her clothes show her body off to its best advantage. She is described as being as slender as a *wezele* (and, as it turns out, as quick-witted and sly as one). She wears over-elaborate clothes which show off her body. In true Chaucerian style this is no doubt indicative of her personality. She is spoken of in terms of the sweet freshness of the countryside. However, all the freshness and beauty hides a much darker side which shows itself in her heartless vulgarity. She is vivacious, skittish and full of sexual energy. All the men in the Tale desire her and she acts as a catalyst for their actions. In the end they all have to endure a painful experience as a result of their desire.

The Miller, Nicholas and Absolon see Alison as a sex object, although Nicholas and Absolon try to disguise their lust in the language they use to her. John sees her as his possession. In spite of her appearance, Alison has not got the class to be more than a yeoman's wife. She hardly needs any persuading to sleep with Nicholas; she lies openly to John telling him that she is faithful, and she supports Nicholas in pretending to the neighbours that John is 'mad'. She is also not beyond indecency, yelling coarsely at Absolon and delighting in the crude joke of sticking her rear end out of the window so that Absolon mistakenly kisses it. Although Alison is very pretty she is far from being like the idealized heroines of courtly romance. Instead she forms part of the comic parody of the courtly love genre in *The Miller's Tale* (see 'Language, style and structure', p. 41).

Nicholas

Nicholas is described as *a poore Scoler* who is making his way through his academic studies at the university and has to rely on financial help from his friends. He also has to find his own accommodation, which suggests that he was from the gentility, rather than the noble classes, who would have provided him with suitable lodgings (see 'The social structure', p. 10). He is boarding with John in order to finish his degree. He is a clever, lively young man and a skilled musician who likes showing off his talent. (Absolon, however, plays an inferior musical instrument and croons in a wavery falsetto.) Nicholas has a passion for astrology. He thinks very well of himself and is proud of his scholarship, arrogantly boasting that *A clerk hadde litherly biset his whyle,/ But if he koude a carpenter bigyle.* We learn that Nicholas knows a good deal about 'secret love', that is, adultery. Because of this he keeps himself to himself, and is sly and deceitful under a superficially charming exterior. He is referred to repeatedly in the tale as *hende* Nicholas. *Hende* would usually mean 'gentle', 'gracious' or 'near at hand', but Nicholas is neither gracious nor courteous. Therefore the word is used ironically to mean 'slick' or 'opportunistic'.

Absolon

Absolon is parish clerk, barber and blood-letter. He is an effeminate and foppish young man who has an eye for the ladies and, like Nicholas, thinks well of himself: *I am a lord at alle degrees.* He especially fancies himself as a hero from a courtly love romances. He seems to take even more care over his appearance than Alison. He has curly, fair hair which he is always combing, and he wears colourful clothes and elaborate shoes. He is extremely fastidious about personal hygiene, taking care that his breath smells sweet, and he has a phobia about smells or people breaking wind – ironic in view of what happens to him later in the Tale. He is described in terms normally associated with women. For instance his eyes are *greye as goos*, and his complexion *reed*, or rosy. He sings in a high falsetto, but ironically takes the part of Herod in the Mystery Plays in order to impress Alison, a role which demands a deep, manly voice. One of his jobs is to swing the censer during church services on Sunday, but instead of religious devotion he spends his time eyeing up the women in the congregation.

Absolon obviously has something of a reputation for fancying himself as a 'womanizer', for not only does the monk at Osney take him to one side to tell him about John's absence, but also Gervase the blacksmith jokes with him about a woman being the cause of his excitement (ironically when in fact Absolon is seeking revenge rather than sexual gratification). Absolon's pretence at chivalry disguises his lust, however. Absolon's absorption with self-image and his obsession with dainty habits make his experiences at the hands of Alison and Nicholas all the more humiliating, and he is determined to get a swift revenge.

Your turn

? Imagine you were going to write a modern-day
   equivalent to *The Canterbury Tales*. Where might you
   set it? Which people from contemporary life might
   you include? Mind Map your ideas.

? Go through this section on characterization circling
   what you consider to be the key words connected
   with the Miller's character and appearance. Do the
   same for each of the other characters. Use different
   colours for each.

Take a well-earned break now!

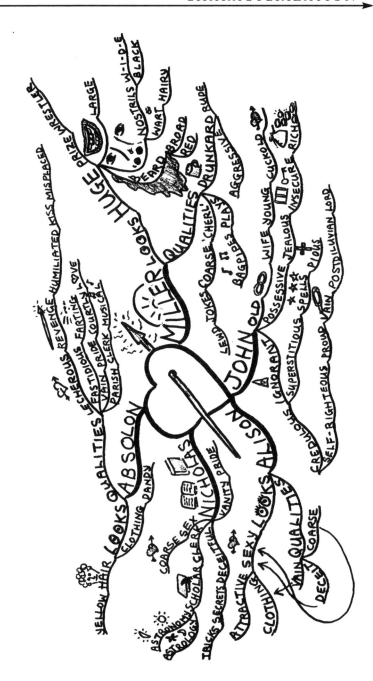

33

THEMES

In *The Miller's Tale* the four main themes of secrecy, ignorance, pride and vanity, and love are closely linked. The main action of the plot hinges on the keeping of secrets, which is then transformed into trickery and deception. If it was not for the ignorance of John, the clever Nicholas would not succeed in using his book learning to dupe John and thereby seduce Alison. All the male characters show themselves to be vain and selfish people who, because of this fault in their natures, suffer apt punishments.

Secrecy and deceit

The theme of secrecy, with the related themes of deceit and trickery, permeate the Tale. For instance, the very first attribute of Nicholas is his fondness for *deerne love* and *solas.* He very much enjoys secret love affairs, and has a strong commitment to physical pleasure. This is a student who balances his academic studies with having a good time! He takes care to keep himself to himself so that he can make the most of his illicit liaisons, but likes to be thought of as a 'good chap', so superficially he seems very respectable, keeping a neat and tidy room and showing off his versatility with nightly musical soirées. (He also may not want the friends who help finance him through college to think badly of him!) Nicholas is attracted to secrecy, and plays on the carpenter's desire to know secrets in order to consummate his *deerne love* for Alison. He is also referred to as *sleigh and ful privee*, again stressing his love of deceit.

Nicholas's love of secrecy sets off a chain of events where all the major characters are involved in the keeping of secrets to a greater or lesser degree. Nicholas keeps his seduction plans secret and tells John that he must not say anything to anyone about the Flood. Alison does a good job of telling John that as she is apparently his good and faithful wife, he must save her – from an imaginary Flood. Both Nicholas and Alison are described as stealing down from their tubs to make love. Absolon manages to keep his revenge secret from Gerveys as well as from Alison and Nicholas. Both Alison and Nicholas are able to manage to fool the neighbours into believing John is mad.

It is not just secular secrets which are mentioned, but also *Goddes privetee*. In the Prologue the Miller mentions that it is not a good idea to know God's secrets, nor is it recommended practice to spy on one's wife: *An housbonde shal nat ben inquisitif/ Of Goddes privetee, nor of his wyf.* The carpenter fears that Nicholas's astrology has in fact been a type of celestial spying for which he will be punished: *This man is falle, with his astromie,/ In some woodnesse or in some agonie./ I thoghte ay wel how that it sholde be!/ Men sholde nat knowe of Goddes privetee.* Nicholas stresses to John that *it is Cristes conseil that I seye* and then swears John to secrecy, ordering him to say nothing to his servants, who apparently will be drowned. He ironically declines to say why this should be – presumably he couldn't think of a good enough reason – but instead declares that *I wol nat tellen Goddes privetee.*

Here we see a show of religious devotion being used to disguise trickery and deceit. Nicholas uses the same ploy a few lines later on when he instructs John to keep absolute silence when he has made the tubs. John, after declaring that it was dangerous to know God's secrets, is now very eager to be privy to the ones Nicholas apparently has: *Sey what thou wolt, I shal it nevere telle/ To child ne wyf, by him that harwed helle!* The irony of course is that Nicholas, the astrologer, could not foretell his own painful branding, and in this sense is just like the scholar John mentions who falls into a clay pit, being too absorbed to notice imminent danger:

> *He walked into the feeldes, for to prye*
> *Upon the sterres, what ther sholde bifalle,*
> *Til he was in a marle-pit yfalle;*
> *He saugh nat that.*

Each of the characters, therefore, John, Nicholas and Absolon, all fail to take adequate precautions to 'look ahead' and see what their actions might precipitate in the future. Pride, vanity and lust blind each of them.

Ignorance and superstition

The fact that Nicholas's trickery works is because he has an advantage over the carpenter in possessing knowledge of astronomy, astrology and theology. Poor old John has a very rudimentary knowledge of any of these academic disciplines; he has seen the consequences of too much study (hence his somewhat self-satisfied anecdote about the astrology student who fell into a clay pit). He is a church-goer, and presumably has seen some of the Mystery Plays. This is, however, not going to give him enough biblical knowledge to know when he is being taken in by a clever manipulator. In addition, like many ignorant folk, he is very superstitious. Whereas Nicholas relies on mathematical and other scientific instruments for his studies, we see John furiously casting strange 'night spells' around the house. John's superstitious and fearful nature makes him the ideal victim. Absolon also has a superstitious side to him. He believes that his itchy mouth and feast dream must indicate an impending sexual conquest. In view of the 'kiss' which he actually *does* experience later, these superstitions are comically ironic.

Absolon, with his romantic dreams and pretensions, also shows himself up to be outdated and foolish. The courtly language he uses sounds very odd coming from his lips. In addition, he totally fails to recognize that Alison is no romantic heroine, nor he a romantic hero! The accomplished and clever Nicholas wins out, and makes Absolon appear all the more deficient and effeminate. In spite of Absolon being trusted by the Church to deal with its legal affairs and parish duties effectively, he is no match for Nicholas – until Nicholas overreaches himself.

Pride and vanity

All the main characters display vanity or pride to a greater or lesser extent, and the male characters get suitably punished for it. Alison is the only character who escapes retribution, but her main pride is in her appearance which she takes care of, probably as a means of attracting lovers more desirable than her ageing husband.

John's vanity is in his pretensions to wisdom, and his desire to have power, co-ruling the earth with Nicholas after the Flood. Nicholas teases John by discussing Solomon, the wise king, and then mentioning John in the same breath: *For thus seith Salomon, that was ful trewe,/ 'Werk al by conseil, and thou shalt nat rewe.'* He goes on to ask John if he has heard of Noah, and John proudly boasts *Yis, ful yoore ago.* Nicholas cunningly leads John by the nose, flattering him: *Men seyn thus, 'Sende the wise, and sey no thing':/ Thou art so wys, it needeth thee nat teche.* He then gives John the awesome responsibility of saving their lives. For John to save a scholar such as Nicholas would indeed be a coup for a carpenter, especially as he has earlier professed *Ye, blessed be alwey a lewed man/ That noght but oonly his bileve kan!*

Nicholas's vanity lies in his intellectual pride. He is a confident young man who knows that he is a talented singer and musician who attracts a lot of admiration. He is also confident enough to know that his advances towards Alison would not seriously be rebuffed, and what is more, he knows what sort of a girl Alison is. Unlike Absolon, he has a grip on the realities of the situation. He is proud of his scholarship. He hugely enjoys gulling the carpenter from the moment that he stirs from his 'trance' to the time that he gives his instructions to John to build the boats. It is only when he decides to go one stage better than Alison that he makes his fatal mistake.

Absolon's vanity lies in his pretensions to be of a higher social status than he is: *I am a lord at alle degrees.* He assumes the role of a courtly lover, like a knight from chivalric romance rather than the parish clerk and town barber. He takes pride in his musicianship, although he sings in a rather effeminate falsetto. He plays Herod in the Mystery Plays to show off to Alison, although the part calls for a deep, commanding voice. He likes to display his dancing abilities: *with his legges casten to and fro,* which gives a picture of ungainly foppery. His clothes are the over-elaborate clothes of a dandy, and his hair and eyes might belong to a courtly heroine rather than a man, gold hair and grey eyes being signs of great female beauty. What makes Absolon even more ridiculous is his over-fastidiousness; his obsession with fresh breath and squeamish attitude to farting. His lust for Alison masquerades as love; his religious duties disguise a lecherous disposition. He is immature and arrogant, and however tolerant of him the monk at Osney Abbey, or Gerveys the blacksmith, appear to be, we know Absolon for what he truly is – a snob who thinks of himself as other than he is, and who is made to look ridiculous. Absolon cries like a beaten child, and has future love-affairs crushed out of existence by the unfortunate 'misplaced kiss'. It would be interesting to consider if he deserves any sympathy.

Love and lust

The Miller's Tale shows a completely different type of love from *The Knight's Tale*. Whereas the rival lovers in the Knight's story are prepared to wait for years in chaste adoration, the rival lovers that the Miller's tells of want a speedy resolution to their sexual desires – as young men often do! Even Absolon thinks that if he gets his kiss: *after this I hope cometh moore.* The eagerness to satisfy carnal desires does not restrict itself to the male characters, as Alison is as eager to jump into bed as he is. However, we may want to ask ourselves if we blame Alison for her conduct as she is bound to an ignorant fool, very much her senior and extremely possessive. Even John, although he claims that he loves Alison and is afraid that she might drown (*allas, myn Alisoun!*), keeps her like a prized

possession in a cage, something he has bought with his riches.

The Miller's story, then, shows us lust and jealousy pretending to be love. We know however that the Miller is the type of man who has absolutely no time for courtly love and all its romantic rituals. By showing us contrasting types of love in the Knight's and Miller's Tales Chaucer is not necessarily being judgemental, but simply showing us different aspects of human love. We should not forget to see that all these different types of love are set against the background of the eternal love of God.

Hint: Remember these themes using the mnemonic **S L I P S**:

S ecrecy

L ove

I gnorance

P ride

S uperstition

Memory Matters

? Make a Mind Map of the literary background to *The Miller's Tale*.

? Draw the theme icons on a piece of paper. Find examples from the text which illustrate these themes.

Language coming up — but take a break first!

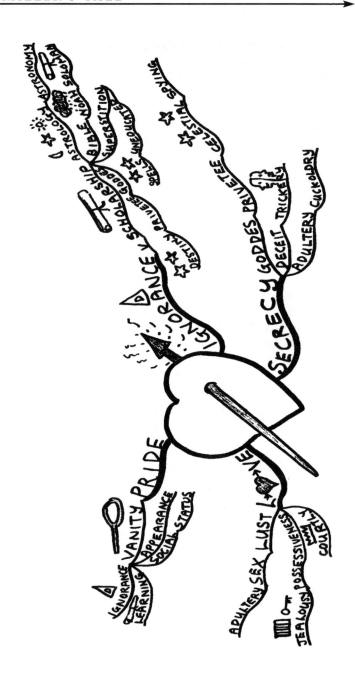

L ANGUAGE, STYLE AND STRUCTURE

Reading aloud

Chaucer's work is part of the oral tradition of English literature in that it is meant to be read aloud. Not many people had access to books and few could even read. Reading therefore was a very important social, rather than a private, activity. There was no such thing as 'silent reading'. Even monasteries, which today we might think of as silent places, would have actually been very noisy. Monks would have read aloud to each other, and would have read aloud even to themselves!

As Chaucer was involved with the court for much of his life, we can assume that the audiences he was writing for included the nobility and even the higher aristocracy, as well as the educated middle class. This cultured audience would be sure to appreciate the subtleties of Chaucer's satire as well as the coarseness of the bawdier tales. We should remember that Chaucer is creating characters whose opinions, methods of argument and words do not necessarily reflect Chaucer's own views. This is why Chaucer warns about the coarseness of the Miller's story in the Prologue, saying that coarseness is only to be expected from a lout like the Miller: *And therefore, whoso list it nat yheere,/ Turne over the leef and chese another tale.* Although *The Canterbury Tales* are meant to be heard aloud, we are to assume from this that an educated audience might have access to it in manuscript form as well.

Poets' debt to Chaucer

Chaucer was the first poet writing in English to use language in such a rich and original way. He would also have made a wonderful dramatist. He introduced ideas and concepts into the Tales which made him an inspiration for all writers who came after him, including Shakespeare. William Caxton, the first English printer, writing in 1478 referred to Chaucer as 'the founder and embellisher of eloquence'. Edmund Spenser, writing in the late sixteenth century, acknowledged his debt to

Chaucer by referring to him as his 'master'. Many of Shakespeare's comic scenes show the influence of Chaucer through their wit, humanity and dramatic energy. John Dryden, poet laureate, writing in the late seventeenth century, referred to Chaucer as 'the father of English poetry', and 'a perpetual fountain of good sense'. Nearer our own time the poet and novelist D. H. Lawrence wrote in 1936, 'Nothing could be more lovely and fearless than Chaucer.'

Chaucer's language

Chaucer is often considered the greatest poet in the English language after Shakespeare, loved for his humanity, wit and wisdom. He was writing at a time when the culture of the English upper classes was predominately French. During Chaucer's lifetime the language used in Parliament changed from French to English, while the clergy and anyone else with education would be able to speak and read Latin.

Chaucer greatly increased the status of English as a literary language. He wrote in what is known as Middle English. The English language had changed over the course of time and was continuing to change in the fourteenth century. Prior to Middle English, Anglo-Saxon, or Old English, would have been spoken. Middle English gradually developed into what we now refer to as Modern English.

Pronunciation

Middle English would have sounded very different from Modern English. In addition, regional dialects were far more in evidence than they are today. Chaucer wrote and spoke the dialect of the East Midlands combined with some influences from London. The pilgrims who started out from the Tabard Inn in Southwark may have heard around them similar accents and dialects, but as they continued towards Canterbury regional differences would have been noticeable. Kent, for example, was often mocked as being 'broad' or 'working class'. This may have been because Kent and Essex were the counties associated with Wat Tyler and the Peasants' Revolt.
✪ How are particular regional accents and dialects stereotyped today?

It is difficult to know exactly how English would have sounded in Chaucer's time, but *The Canterbury Tales* is about as good a piece of evidence as we are likely to get. Chaucer was very aware of the changes that the English language was going through. In a startling, almost prophetic insight, he tells us:

> *Ye knowe ek that in forme of speche is chaunge*
> *Withinne a thousand yeer, and wordes tho*
> *That hadden pris, now wonder nyce and straunge*
> *Us thinketh hem, and yet thei spake hen so.*
> *Troilus and Criseyde*, Prologue, Book 11

Chaucer was writing in poetry. The Prologues and Tales are full of very believable characters whose stories, whether funny or sad, are full of action. We could say then, that *The Canterbury Tales* are in fact poems written as dramatic narratives (stories with plenty of dramatic action).

RHYMING COUPLETS

Chaucer wrote most of *The Canterbury Tales* in rhyming couplets (a pair of rhyming lines). That is, in each pair of lines, the lines end with a word which rhymes. Take these two lines from *The Miller's Tale:*

> *But sith that he was fallen in the snare,*
> *He mooste endure, as oother folk, his care.*

The words *snare* and *care* rhyme with each other. The Tales themselves are so skilfully told that it is not immediately obvious that we are listening to rhyming couplets. Instead we are swept away with feeling that surely we are listening to real characters speaking with colloquial liveliness.

IAMBIC PENTAMETER

This is verse with five pairs of syllables to a line, with the stress always on the second syllable. Chaucer was the first poet in English to write in iambic pentameter, a rhythm or metre (rhythm or beats in lines of verse, created by regulated groups of syllables) which became very popular. This simply means that each line has five groups of syllables with the stress falling on the second syllable. When you read the lines through aloud, you will be able to count five 'beats' in each line:

But sith that he was fallen in the snare,
He mooste endure, as oother folk, his care.

SPEAKING THE VERSE

In Chaucer's time, the final 'e' in words like *sette* and *dette* was often pronounced (though usually not when the next word began with a vowel or an 'h'). They would have therefore sounded rather as the Modern English 'setter' and 'debtor'. In addition, words beginning with the letter 'y', such as ywroght would be pronounced like the 'y' in the modern 'courtly'. The syllables in words such as *housbondes* would also be sounded out separately as if you were saying the phrase, 'whose bond is'. Here is a couplet from *The Miller's Tale* (lines 267–8)

He woweth hire by meenes and brocage,
And swoor he wolde been hire owene page.

In this couplet *meenes* has two syllables and *brocage* has three, so that they would be pronounced 'mean-is' and 'bro-ca-zhur' (sounding like the French). The words *wolde*, *owene* and *page* would have two syllables each, as in 'would -er ', 'own-er' and 'pah-zhur'.

Hint: If in doubt, pronounce all letters in a word, but not a final 'e' if the next word begins with a vowel or an 'h'.

Over to you

? Listen to a recording of a professional reading of Chaucer. You should be able to get one from a bookshop or library.

? Choose a section of the Tale which describe John's fears about Nicholas and his studies, such as lines 343–4. Working with a partner or in a small group, take it in turns to read these lines aloud. One student could clap the rhythm. See if you can make each line sound different, for example, fearful, despairing or 'knowing'.

Take a break before your next look at language.

Language and characterization

The Canterbury Tales presents us with characters who are made to reveal their personalities not only through what they say but also by the way they tell their stories. Chaucer is adept at reproducing the rhythms and vocabulary of colloquial (the language of ordinary conversation) English. The effect of this is to make us feel we are actually listening to fourteenth-century conversation. This is just an illusion however; no character, particularly one as rough and ready as the drunken Miller, would have been able to talk in the regular metre Chaucer was writing in, let alone rhyming couplets! But such is the mastery of Chaucer's poetic style that we are carried along with the sheer energy and vibrancy of the language.

The language in *The Miller's Tale* is often dramatic and full of colloquial expressions. For example, the Miller, who is used to telling dirty jokes, speaks openly and bluntly about Alison's sexuality. He describes Alison as *a primerole, a piggesnie* and a *popelote*, the repeated plosive 'p' sounds suggest sexuality and sexual excitement.

The Miller vulgarly refers to Absolon's misplaced kiss as *Absolon hath kist hir nether ye*, a euphemism (covering an unpleasant fact by using a much milder term) which no doubt would make his audience laugh. All the characters – John, Alison, Nicholas, Absolon and Gervase – are fond of using expletives (swear words) and exclamations in their speech. Nicholas says he will die unless Alison agrees to sleep with him – *also God me save* – and delights in Absolon's misplaced kiss – *A berd! a berd! quod hende Nicholas,/ By Goddes corpus, this goth faire and weel*. As a contrast there are the outmoded expressions which Absolon uses, based on courtly love, such as *I praye yow that ye wole rewe on me*.

The language which all the characters speak gives strong impressions of their personalities. For instance, John in his ignorance mispronounces words, referring to *Nowelis* flood, and *astromie*, and Gervase, albeit having a cameo role, shows himself to possess bluff jocularity. Alison's coarse nature – in contrast with her outward appearance – is also revealed in her crude put-downs of Absolon.

Proverbs

The Miller's Tale is full of proverbial expressions and sayings. Most of these are told by the narrator – the Miller – in which he is making a comment about the characters or the situation. Examples of these include:

> *He knew nat Catoun, for his wit was rude,*
> *That bad man sholde wedde his similitude.*
> *Me sholde wedden fater hire estaat,*
> *For youthe and elde is often at debaat.*

Here, the Miller is commenting on the marriage of John and Alison. The wooing of Alison by Absolon is also commented on: *For som folk wol ben wonnen for richesse,/ And somme for strokes, and somme for gentillesse.* Nicholas's 'handy' proximity is compared with Absolon's more distant rivalry: *Men seyn right thus, 'Alwey the nie slie/ Maketh the ferre leeve to be looth.* John's credulousness in the face of Alison's protestations that he must save her from the Flood provokes the following philosophical reflection which is rather less the Miller's than Chaucer himself:

> *Lo, which a greet thing is affeccioun!*
> *Men may dyen of imaginacioun,*
> *So depe may impressioun be take.*

Alliteration and onomatopoeia

Alliteration is the repetition of a sound at the beginning of words or syllables, e.g. *His rode was reed.* Chaucer uses alliteration to enhance the meaning and effect of his lines. This involves choosing to use words beginning with the same consonant to create a pattern of sounds, e.g. *Into the roof they kiken and they cape.* Here the curiosity of the neighbours peering and craning to see into the rafters of the house is enhanced by 'k' sounds which suggests the jerky movements of heads and necks, as well as excited chatter.

Onomatopoeia is the use of words whose sounds help to suggest the meaning, e.g. *thonder-dent*, e.g. *For travaille of his goost he groneth soore.* This description of John's restlessness as he eventually falls asleep in the uncomfortable position in the tub after his exertions and worry is emphasized by the repeated 'g' sounds on 'goost' and 'groneth'. The words 'goost', 'groneth' and 'soore' are also onomatopoeic in that the 'oo' sounds in all three words suggests the moans of the troubled carpenter in his sleep.

Imagery

Chaucer uses imagery to make his descriptions more vivid. In particular he uses **similes**, comparing two usually unrelated things, e.g. *softer than the wolle is of a wether*. The imagery he uses in *The Miller's Tale* falls into several categories.

COUNTRYSIDE

Images of the countryside are used to describe Alison in what is essentially a parody of the courtly love genre. Instead of a portrait extolling the virtues of a noble lady, we are not allowed to forget that, for all her charms, Alison is a still a simple country wench, the heroine of a rustic comedy. Alison's eyebrows are described as being black as sloes; her general appearance as attractive as a pear tree in full blossom. Her breath is *sweete as bragot or the meeth,/ Or hoard of apples leyd in hey or heeth*. Her apron is *as whit as morne milk;* her face is scrubbed and radiant after her work as a country girl's would be; she is as pretty as wild flowers: *She was a primerole, a piggesnie.*

ANIMALS

Alison's nature is revealed to the reader partly through the references to animals. Her body is compared with a *wezele*, a fast-moving, lithe and sly creature. She is also *softer than the wolle is of a wether.* She sings and chatters like a swallow sitting on a barn, and is playful and skittish as a colt, a kid and calf: *She sproong as a colt dooth in the trave.* Animal imagery is also used to describe Absolon, although the animals chosen are more like those chosen to describe female heroines: *His eyen greye as goos*; *He singeth, brokkinge as a nightingale.* Absolon's predatory feelings towards Alison as he gazes on her in church is described in terms of a cat stalking a mouse: *I dar wol seyn if she hadde been a mous,/ And he a cat, he wolde hire hente anon.* Absolon's longing for Alison is described by him as resembling *a lamb after the tete.* Nicholas refers to Alison floating happily after John in her tub after the 'Flood' as *the white doke after hire drake.*

Being a wonderful persuader, Nicholas is deliberately trying here to put across an image to John which conjures up not only a picture of security, but also suggests Alison's wifely obedience, something John would dearly like to be sure of!

BLACK AND WHITE/ LIGHT AND DARKNESS

Alison's appearance is also described in images of black and white. Her complexion, which is bright and radiant, contrasts with her hair, which is as dark as sloes. Her apron falls fetchingly over her white smock, which is set off by her black silk collar. Her cap matches her smock, but the ribbons which secure it are also black:

> *... on hir coler aboute,*
> *Of col-blak silk, withinne and eek withoute.*
> *The tapes of hir white voluper*
> *Were of the same suite of hir coler.*

As well as being a pleasing combination of colours, which suggest Alison's prettiness and her attempts at elegance, the contrasting colours also remind us that although Alison appears angelic on the outside, she has another 'darker' side to her nature which she reveals in her attitude towards John and Absolon.

Images of light and dark permeate the Tale. Night is the time of love and sensuality. Nicholas plays and sings, *a-nightes melodie.* Absolon goes courting for the first time by the light of the moon: *The moone, whan it was night, ful brighte shoon.* Nicholas and Alison consummate their desires at night. But the night also has a sinister aspect. Nicholas is found staring at the moon when he is putting into play his trickery, and John weaves a night-spell to exorcize any demons Nicholas's star-gazing has brought on the house. The pretend Flood is due to arrive at night and the rains to stop the following morning. Alison, John and Nicholas creep into their tubs at night, and John extinguishes all the candles in his house as part of his preparations. Night is the time when Alison humiliates Absolon: *Derk was the night as pich, or as the cole*. It is when Nicholas breaks wind in Absolon's face and when he receives Absolon's excruciating revenge. The fart itself is described as a *thonder-dent*, which suggests a dark thunderstorm!

If the night is 'active', that is, when most of the action happens, then the day is 'passive', in that the coming of the morning light is a time of revelation. For example, in the cold light of day the events of the night are exposed. Absolon tells Gervase, who enquires why Absolon wants the hot coulter, *I shal wel telle it thee to-morwe day*. The very next day John is humbled in front of the townsfolk, and Nicholas's branded backside will no doubt be discovered! Alison scrubs her face after her work before going to church: *Hir forheed shoon as bright as any day*. Alison, who always wants to impress through her external appearance, scrubs away any taint from her complexion before going to church, but cannot do the same for her 'tainted' personality, having gone to Mass immediately after making the pact with Nicholas. (We might also wonder if God would object to good, honest sweat!) Absolon, who strives towards the romantic ideal, finds his ambition thwarted by the presence of Nicholas: *This nie Nicholas stood in his light*. We still talk about 'standing in someone's shadow'.

Many of the characters in the Tale have 'light and dark' sides to their personalities. Alison appears pretty, pure and innocent, but is vulgar and lustful underneath. Nicholas appears to be a 'model' student, keeping his living quarters neat and his private life private, but he is in reality arrogant and deceitful. Absolon apes being a gentleman of refinement and has a position of trust in the church. He abuses his position, is ridiculously pretentious, and reveals himself to be nothing but a rather immature lecher! John claims to love Alison, but his love 'imprisons' her. He also has ideas above his station and is flattered at the thought of being a post-diluvian ruler. His reputation is all-important to him and yet at the end of the Tale it is in tatters.

TASTE AND SMELL

Absolon's fussiness about smell and taste are shown in the references to both these senses. He refers to Alison as *honycomb* and *sweete cinamome*. He sends her gifts of spiced ale and cakes and chews liquorice before he visits her. After his 'misplaced kiss' we are asked in a rhetorical question (a question which is a figure of speech and demands no answer, or no answer is expected): *Who rubbeth now, who froteth now his lippes/ With dust, with sond, with straw, with clooth, with chippes, But Absolon* ....This, of course enhances the comedy, as Absolon's fastidiousness in these areas has been well documented throughout the Tale.

FACT FILE

Your exam answer will be improved if you can identify and discuss the effectiveness of Chaucer's use of imagery, rhythm and rhyme.

Links between the Prologue and Tale

The Prologue provides a means whereby a transition can take place from one storyteller to the next. In this case the Knight has finished his Tale and the Miller insists on telling his Tale next. This will be a comic contrast to the Knight's, despite references to the Miller's own 'noble story'. The Prologue therefore contains much information about the Knight's story and the story that will come next. The fact that the Miller's character is also revealed in the Prologue suggests to the audience what kind of tale to expect from him. This is emphasized by the conflict between the Miller and Host, and the Miller and the Reeve, as well as by the final disowning of the Miller's story by the narrator! Of course, it is very intriguing to be told to turn to another Tale as this one might displease in some way, so perhaps this long disclaimer is also a subtle device on the part of Chaucer to engage his audience's interest!

How does The Miller's Tale *fit in with the other Tales?*

The Miller insisted on telling his Tale after the Knight's instead of letting the Monk tell his story (which would have been the polite and socially acceptable thing to do.) *The Miller's Tale,* following the Knight's story of courtly love, is a wonderful parody of that genre. In addition, the subversive quality of *The Miller's Tale*, showing, as it does, a respectable man made to look foolish, suits the roguish Miller! There are suggestions that perhaps – *just perhaps* – the pilgrims did not unanimously think that the Knight's story was wonderful. Notice how it is *namely the gentils everichon* who are mentioned as approving the Knight's tale. There are after all, others in the company who might indeed prefer the sort of entertainment the Miller's story provides! Remember that there are layers and layers of meanings to Chaucer's poetry. Like 'Chinese boxes', nothing is what it seems on the surface – look closely at one meaning and you just might uncover another!

The Reeve's Tale was designed by the Reeve to get his own back on the Miller and therefore follows *The Miller's Tale.* This story is another fabliau, full of ribald humour, and tells of how a roguish Miller is cuckolded and beaten.

Parody

The Miller's Tale is an example of parody (i.e. it mimics or apes another genre for humorous effect). In this case the genre is 'courtly love' and in this particular instance, *The Knight's Tale.* The Tale the Miller tells is the mirror image of the Knight's. *The Knight's Tale* is serious in tone with rather a gloomy vision of the world, whereas *The Miller's Tale* is essentially joyous in spite of the painful come-uppances! The Knight deals with aristocratic characters – knights and dukes – whereas the Miller deals with ordinary folk such as carpenters and local barbers. *The Knight's Tale* shows love as being undemanding and expecting nothing, in the true chivalric tradition, but *The Miller's Tale* shows lust masquerading as love, and a burlesque of courtly love. *The Knight's Tale* shows philosophical questioning of divine justice; *The Miller's Tale* shows 'rough' justice. The heightened language that the Knight's uses is replaced by the colloquial and often coarse language of the Miller. The fact that the effeminate Absolon tries to use the language of courtly love but does not realize that it is already out-of-date (and in any case it is rather odd in the mouth of a barber and parish clerk) makes this aspect of the Tale all the more absurd. The wedded bliss of Palamon and Emily in *The Knight's Tale* is replaced in *The Miller's Tale* by the mismatched marriage of John and Alison.

Emily, the 'ideal' heroine, is described in terms that match the medieval concept of perfect female beauty: *That Emelye, that fairer was to sene/ Than is the lylie upon his stalke grene.* Her complexion is described in terms of roses, and her voice like that of an angel. Her only adornment is a garland of red and white flowers. Alison, the carpenter's wife, has to improve her appearance by plucking her eyebrows (something a heroine of courtly romances would not have to do being already the model of perfection), and makes herself attractive by emphasizing her sexuality with suggestive clothing and showy brooches. She does not possess an angel's voice, but instead chatters like a swallow. Alison is a country girl, and the imagery used to describe her reflects this. Emily on the other hand walks in an elegant, cultivated garden. Similarly, Nicholas provides the audience with a travesty of a courtly lover, as he is certainly not prepared to wait years like Palamon or Arcite in order to win his lady's favour!

Whereas Oxford and the surrounding hamlets provides the homely location for the Miller's story, by contrast the Knight sets his tale in and around an exotic Athenian court, presided over ultimately by gods and goddesses.

Hint: There is evidence from Chaucer's manuscript that he deliberately intended *The Miller's Tale* to be placed after *The Knight's Tale* and before *The Reeve's Tale*. To increase your understanding it is therefore extremely important that you take time to read both these tales in order to compare them with *The Miller's Tale*, and to see how these first three Tales relate to each other as part of *The Canterbury Tales*.

How does Chaucer make the plot credible?

Chaucer makes an implausible plot believable by including realistic details of location, setting and time. The place he has chosen is Oxford, a well-known university town, and we are also told of the nearby town of Osney, with its abbey and outlying farmsteads.

We are given a detailed description of John's house, its doors, windows, roof-beams and cat hole, and a description of the surrounding neighbourhood. We know of Gervase the blacksmith, whose forge is just across the street, the local church where Absolon eyes up the local women, and the taverns where he plays his *giterne*. Nicholas's room is also described in detail, where his treasured books and scientific instruments are, and where his dulcimer lies on a red cloth.

Chaucer is very careful to ensure that the gulling of the carpenter takes place within a logical time frame. Hence we are told that on Saturday the plan was hatched, and Nicholas stays in his room until Sunday evening. We are also told that the Flood would come the next Monday and the Flood waters abate the following morning. We know that Alison and Nicholas creep down from their tubs at 'curfew time' and sleep together until 'lauds' the following day.

The plot itself runs smoothly: Nicholas disappears, apparently has a 'revelation' and is believed by a credulous and superstitious man who is flattered with the idea of being singled out as a second Noah. Absolon's persistent courtship leads on to his humiliation with effortless ease, and Absolon's revenge, with the resultant cries for *'Water!'* leads seamlessly on to the carpenter's literal, as well as metaphorical downfall, 'water' being a trigger word for what is foremost in the carpenter's mind.

Narrative voice

Chaucer meant this story to be spoken aloud. Consequently, throughout this tale we are aware of the storyteller's voice occasionally breaking into the narrative. Sometimes there are direct comments on the actions or attitudes of the characters: *Men sholde wedden after hire estaat,/ For youthe and elde is often at debaat*. The Miller here offers further opinions about marriage in addition to the ones already voiced in the Prologue. Absolon's predatory infatuation with Alison is also commented on:

> *I dar wel seyn if she hadde been a mous,*
> *And he a cat, he wolde hire hente anon;*
> *This parissh clerk, this amorous Absolon,*
> *That is for love alwey so wo bigon.*

Sometimes the narrator will make a wise remark: *Lo, which a greet thing is affeccioun!* At other times the characters are addressed: *Now ber thee wel, thou hende Nicholas,/ For Absolon may waille and singe 'allas'.* This direct addressing of Nicholas has the effect of injecting an extra dimension of realism into the Tale. The audience is therefore always being subtly involved in the narrative. At other times the characters are allowed to speak for themselves:

> *Allas!*
> *My soul bitake I unto Sathanas,*
> *But me were levere than al I this toun*
> *Of this despit awroken for to be.*

Although it is sometimes rather hard to believe that a man such as the Miller would be prone to philosophical reflection or references to *'Catoun'*, it is also amusing to consider how a drunken *cherl* might speak Alison's gleeful *Teehee!* or Absolon's *Spek, sweete brid, I noot nat where thou art*. At the end of the Tale the main points of the story are summarized neatly and without need for further elaboration:

> *Thus swived was this carpenteris wyf,*
> *For al his keping and his jalousie;*
> *And Absolon hath kist hir nether ye;*
> *And Nicholas is scalded in the towte.*

No moral judgement is made, and the storyteller merely takes his 'bow' before the assembled company: *This tale is doon, and God save al the rowte.*

Pace and shifts of focus

Compared with the elegant, slow-moving pace of *The Knight's Tale*, the pace of *The Miller's Tale* alternately speeds up and slows down. The motionless Nicholas, seated in his room staring at the moon, is preceded by the frenetic activity of the Miller and his servant breaking down the door:

> *His knave was a strong carl for the nones,*
> *And by the hasp he haaf it of atones;*
> *Into the floor the dore fil anon.*
> *This Nicholas sat ay as stille as stoon,*
> *And evere caped upward into the eir.*

John's hectic flood preparations, *he gooth and geteth him a kneding trogh,/ And after that a tubbe and a kymelin*, are followed by the leisurely courtship preparations of Absolon:

> *Up riste this joly lovere Absolon,*
> *And him arraieth gay, at point-devis.*
> *But first he cheweth greyn and licoris,*
> *To smellen sweete, er he hadde kembd his heer.*

From then on the plot speeds up to culminate in the climax of the carpenter's downfall.

The focus of the plot constantly shifts from character to character throughout the Tale. For example, firstly the emphasis is on Nicholas and his successful seduction of Alison. Then we are presented with Absolon and his unsuccessful wooing. The focus then shifts once more to concentrate on the plot to dupe the carpenter, before returning again to Absolon. This shifting pattern of focus continues until the end of the Tale, giving it a cinematic quality.

Power, too, also alters between the characters. At first Nicholas has his own way and is accomplishing his desires, then he is joined by Alison, and the two of them combine to torment Absolon. With Absolon's revenge the tables are turned. When the carpenter hears Nicholas's shouts and falls to the floor Alison and Nicholas quickly succeed in rescuing the situation by discrediting the carpenter in the eyes of his neighbours.

It will be noticed that there are certain 'continuity problems' in the Tale. For instance, after entry to Nicholas's room has been gained by getting Robin to wrest the door from its hinges, we are told a few lines later that when the carpenter returns with ale, *This Nicholas his dore faste shette.* Similarly, after Nicholas's branding and the excruciating pain that resulted, *and for the smert he wende for to die*, we see him almost immediately afterwards having recovered enough to rush into the street with Alison, proclaiming John's 'madness' to the astonished neighbourhood. These anomalies do not detract from the plot – after all the Tale was meant to be heard, rather than read, and the plot is engaging. Such is Chaucer's skill then, that these 'slips' may well go unnoticed, and if they *are* stumbled upon they simply do not matter!

Music and religion

Music and religion permeate the Tale. Sometimes they can be separated from each other, but on the whole, in this Tale they are indivisible. Each of the three protagonists, Alison, Nicholas and Absolon, are described in connection with music. Alison's enthusiastic and lively singing is compared with the noisy chattering of swallows. Nicholas has a treasured dulcimer and he plays and sings well, usually at night, such works as *The King's Note* and *Angelus ad virginem,* a joyous melody which still survives today. This song, although referring to the Angel Gabriel's appearance to the Virgin Mary has ironic overtones, as Nicholas will later accost Alison when her husband (also a carpenter) is out!

Absolon also plays and sings, but in contrast with Nicholas he seems to find it necessary to go out and seek an audience in the local inns. Absolon plays an instrument called a *giterne*, a stringed instrument like a guitar and possibly less complicated to master than Nicholas's *sautrie*. Absolon's voice seems to be inferior to Nicholas's as we are given the impression of a tremulous falsetto, no doubt to contrast with Nicholas's manly tenor or baritone. When Nicholas and Alison spend the night together, the audience hears that they did not speak to each other, instead they 'made music together' in their lovemaking: *Ther was the revel and the melodie.*

Chaucer goes on to say that they made love, *Til that the belle of laudes gan to ringe,/ And freres in the chauncel gonne singe.* The monks begin to sing praises at the first Mass of the day and, because of the juxtaposition of the secular and religious subject matter, they ironically seem to be celebrating Nicholas's successful seduction rather than a religious observance! Notice also that through the Tale religion is subverted for the ends of the unscrupulous rivals, Nicholas and Absolon. Nicholas uses the story of the Flood to prey upon the ignorance and fear of the carpenter. Absolon uses his position in the Church as a hunting ground for potential sexual partners. As both these characters are clerks then it might be that Chaucer is making a statement about the power and influence of the Church over ordinary people. However, as always, Chaucer's political allegiances remain elusive. England in the fourteenth century could be a dangerous place for dissenters.

Morality and values in the Tale

In the Prologue the Miller says that he will tell *a noble tale* which would *quite* the Knight's story, which it may well do on entertainment value! A 'noble tale' is not exactly what we are presented with. However, Chaucer reminds us that the Miller is a rough fellow, and if we expect moral lessons or gentility we can turn to other Tales for these qualities. Chaucer also says that he has to faithfully report what the Miller says, and the Miller shows us ordinary people who are flawed, behaving in often outrageous ways, just as the human race is flawed and can sometimes behave outrageously. Their behaviour is neither recommended nor condemned.

After the Miller has finished his story we learn that although some of the company grumbled, especially the Reeve, the majority dissolved in laughter. This would indicate that even if *The Miller's Tale* did not supply an overt moral, that it was well received by the Pilgrims. But does *The Miller's Tale* offer a moral for us? The Miller's brief summary at the end of his story would indicate not. However, Chaucer was writing from a Christian viewpoint and often shows his characters behaving impiously against a pious background. For instance, Alison visits the church not long after making her love-pact with Nicholas; Nicholas sings *Angelus ad virginem* before accosting

Alison; Absolon eyes up the congregation in his role as parish clerk and checks with the monks at Osney abbey to find out where John is, and Nicholas and Alison make love to the sounds of the monks singing God's praises.

❂ How far do you sympathize with each of the characters?

In the Tale we are presented with a variety of sins such as lust, adultery, possessiveness, deceit, pride, vanity and revenge. The three male characters are all victims of vanity and pride, and receive fitting punishments. For instance, John pretends to be wise and is pleased to be privy to 'divine' information about the 'Flood'. He also quite likes the idea of being a post-diluvian lord with unlimited power over his wife and what might be left of life on earth. He is extremely jealous with Alison. His punishment therefore is to be cuckolded, in spite of his best efforts, to be made to look like a fool, to suffer a broken arm and to lose the respect of the local community.

Absolon shows himself to be both pretentious and stubborn by firstly aping a courtly love image and then by refusing to abandon it. His punishment is to be humiliated in a manner which reflects his deepest loathings. Nicholas also shows us he has intellectual vanity and pride. Although he manages to dupe the carpenter, he makes the mistake of trying to outdo Alison in the taunting of Absolon. He also receives his punishment – a painful burn on his rear end with a hot coulter. This punishment has been regarded as a parody of chivalric duelling, or a comic version of Satan's branding of souls in the fires of hell, a visual image often found in contemporary fourteenth-century woodcuts or stone carvings.

Only Alison escapes being punished (unless losing the carpenter could be seen as a punishment). Possibly this is because she is the only character who does not pretend to be cleverer than she is. In addition, she plays a passive role in the trickery, but nevertheless remains constantly wily.

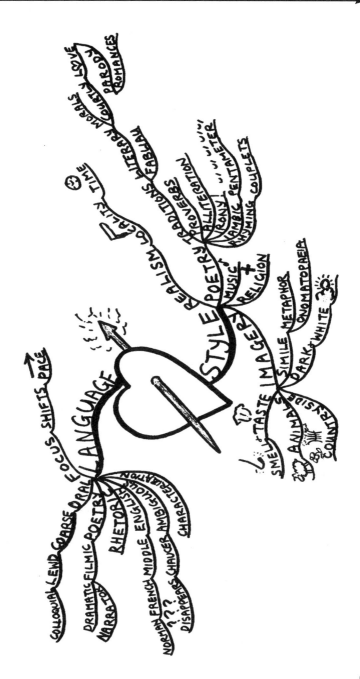

COMMENTARY ON THE PROLOGUE

The Miller's Prologue

Lines 1, *Whan that the Knight had thus his tale ytoold,* to 78, *And eek men shal nat maken ernest of game.*

- ◆ The Knight's tale is well received.
- ◆ The Miller insists he should tell his Tale next.
- ◆ The Host and the Reeve object.
- ◆ The Miller has his way, and Chaucer disassociates himself from the ensuing Tale.

THE NOBLE STORY OF THE KNIGHT

The Knight's Tale is well received by the company, especially the gentlefolk, who all consider it to be *a noble storie.* Now that the storytelling has begun, the Host, Harry Bailly, landlord of the Tabard Inn at Southwark, looks at the band of pilgrims and asks the Monk to tell his tale, presumably because he is next in social status to the Knight.

THE MUZZY MOUTHINGS OF THE MILLER

Robin, the Miller, interrupts. He is obviously very drunk, and is even finding it difficult to sit on the saddle of his horse. This is not the sort of man who is prepared to defer out of courtesy to anybody, and he makes a point of refusing to take off his hat and hood before addressing the company. Shouting in a loud and threatening way, he says that he has *a noble tale* which will outmatch the Knight's. Despite the best efforts of the Host, the Miller insists on telling his story, threatening to leave the company if he is prevented from doing so. The Host reluctantly gives in.

I TELL A GOOD TALE – ON SOUTHWARK ALE!

The Miller openly admits he is drunk, blaming his slurred speech and any mispronunciations on the beer he had to drink at Southwark. He says he intends to tell the story of a

60

carpenter and his wife, and of a student who made a fool of the carpenter. ✪ What opinion have you formed of the Miller so far?

THE CARPENTER WITH A CHIP ON HIS SHOULDER

Oswald, the Reeve, immediately objects to the Miller's proposed story as *lewed dronken harlotrie*, anticipating a bawdy and obscene tale. After all, the Reeve is also a carpenter and therefore has his own interests at heart. He says the Miller has no right to damage the reputation of any man or his wife, although he is welcome to speak on another subject to his heart's content.

NO SLEAZE, IF YOU PLEASE!

The Miller quickly responds to the Reeve, and denies that he is calling anyone a cuckold. He adds, rather sarcastically, that for every bad woman there are a thousand good ones, so why should the Reeve be angry with his choice of subject matter? The Miller then declares that *he* does not believe that his own wife has cuckolded him, not that he would enquire too closely into the matter. After all, he states, both a wife's privacy, and God's secrets should not be investigated too closely.

IF THE MILLER'S TALE IS COARSER, DON'T BLAME IT ON CHAUCER

The Miller will not be silenced, and so prepares to tell his bawdy story to the assembled company. Chaucer appeals to his audience not to be offended, stating that since the Miller is a churlish fellow, a coarse tale is only to be expected. After all, adds Chaucer, there are plenty of tales told by the other pilgrims which contain gentility, morality and holiness, unlike the scurrilous tales of the Miller and the Reeve. However, he says he is bound to give a faithful account of all the stories told. Chaucer continues by asking his audience to turn to another Tale if they are unhappy, and not to take seriously what is meant in fun.

✒ STYLE AND LANGUAGE

Throughout the Prologue, Chaucer builds up a picture of the Miller which prepares the audience for the ribaldry and licentiousness of his Tale. Chaucer can therefore apologize for the Tale and say that it suited a rough fellow like the Miller, who *tolde his cherles tale in his manere.* The poet Chaucer can therefore 'disappear' inside his own text, something Chaucer is very fond of doing. In these lines the poet steps aside and actually addresses his audience directly, instead of leaving the stage to his characters.

Although the Miller states that he will tell *a noble tale for the nones,* his ensuing Tale will prove the irony of this comment. In addition, it is doubtful whether the Miller really holds any respect for female virtue when he states: *Ther been ful goode wives many oon,/ And evere a thousand goode ayens oon badde.* It is likely, given the events of his Tale, that this comment is sarcastic! Also, the Miller has no love for the Reeve, whom he refers to as *Leve brother Osewold,* sentiments that the Miller certainly does not mean. The Reeve later retaliates with his Tale about a rascally miller who was cuckolded.

The Miller may well suspect his own wife has been unfaithful, but will not *Take upon me moore than ynogh,* and try to prove it. He will just *bileve wel that I am noon,* quoting his maxim, *An housbonde shal nat ben inquisitif/ Of Goddes privetee, nor of his wyf.* The themes of infidelity and not prying into God's secrets are later repeated in the Tale.

Your turn

- ? Pick out words and phrases which might engage a reader's interest in the ensuing Tale.
- ? Begin a Mini Mind Map of the character and appearance of the Miller.

COMMENTARY ON THE TALE

Section 1

Lines 79, *Whilsom ther was dwellinge at Oxenford*, to 112, *After his freendes finding and his rente*.

- ◆ The Miller introduces John, the carpenter, and Nicholas, his lodger.
- ◆ Nicholas's lifestyle is described.

THE OLD CODGER AND THE YOUNG LODGER

The Miller describes how John, a carpenter living in Oxford, lets his room to Nicholas, a student who has a passion for astrology. He is adept at making predictions about the weather and auspicious days through his astrological calculations (see 'Astrologie, astronomye, p. 9). ✪ John is described as a *rich gnof*. In what ways does this set up the reader's first impressions of the carpenter?

A SLY, SECRETIVE STUDENT

We are told that this gracious young man knows a good deal about secret love affairs and derives much enjoyment from them. However, he presents himself as someone who keeps himself to himself, appearing modest and retiring.

THE BEGUILING BACHELOR'S BEDSIT

Nicholas lives alone in his room which he decorates with fragrant herbs, and he also likes to keep himself smelling sweet. He has several books in his room including a copy of Ptolemy's *Almageste*, and he also has an astrolabe which he uses for his astrological calculations. On shelves above his bed he keeps his treasured *augrim stones*, or calculation counters. He has draped a coarse red cloth over a cupboard, and on it is placed his dulcimer. At night he sings and accompanies himself on this instrument so well, that the room echoes with the sounds of *Angelus ad virginem* or *The King's Note*, and anyone who hears him admires his musicianship. In this way the 'charming' student spends his days, living on his own income and his friends' charitable handouts. ✪ How does Chaucer set the scene for Nicholas's affair?

✎ STYLE AND LANGUAGE

Nicholas is referred to as *hende* throughout the text, the term meaning 'courteous', 'chivalric' or 'gentle'. However, Nicholas is far from being any of these things, and the word subsequently acquires ironic overtones. Nicholas's love of secrecy is also introduced in this section through words and phrases such as *deerne love* and *privee.* He is also described as *meke*, a word which belies the true nature of his character, as Nicholas intends to look like the ideal lodger when he is in fact lusting after his landlord's wife. Nicholas likes to impress with his culture and artistic abilities, and the words *swetely*, *mirie throte* and *blessed* show his pride in his singing voice. We are also told that he sings at night, *a-nightes melodie*, a time when people would hear his songs to their best advantage as night time is the 'romantic' time to sing. We are also told that Nicholas is partly supported financially by his friends. No doubt Nicholas gives them the outward impression of being charming and gentlemanly also!

Section 2

Lines 113, *This carpenter hadde wedded newe a wyf*, to 162, *Or yet for any good yeman to wedde*

◆ We are introduced to the carpenter's wife.
◆ Alison is described.

A JEALOUSLY GUARDED GIRL

The old carpenter jealously guards his new wife, 18-year-old Alison, as he is afraid she will be unfaithful to him. However, the Miller says he should have known better than to marry one so young and headstrong!

LUSCIOUS, LIVELY AND LECHEROUS

Alison is a very pretty girl. The Miller describes her as wearing silk, an expensive material not usually worn by wenches of her class. Her belt is striped in silk, as is the embroidery on a headband which she sets high on her head. She also has silk embroidery on both the back and front of her smock. Even the strings of her white cap are embroidered with silk. Over her smock she wears a large, white, gored apron, which rests on her thighs. Her collar, of charcoal black silk, is cut low and set off by a large brooch. She wears high-laced boots and a girdle, from which hangs her purse, which is studded with brass beads and has silk tassels hanging from it. According to the Miller, Alison had a sexily suggestive way of looking. She has plucked her eyebrows, which are as *blake as any sloo,* and her complexion is as bright and shining as a newly minted coin.

As far as her temperament goes, we are told that she is lively, quick and full of fun, and as skittish and playful as a young colt. Her body is as slender as a weasel's, and she stands tall and upright. In short she was an irresistible *popelote*, blessed with sweet breath and a lively, loud singing voice. She would make a good mistress for a lord, the Miller tells us, or a good wife for any yeoman! ❷ Alison's apron is described as *whit as morne milk.* The simile expresses freshness and wholesomeness. In what ways might this be ironic?

🖊 STYLE AND LANGUAGE

Chaucer prepares us for the inevitable seduction of the newly wedded Alison as he mentions the old carpenter's fear that he may *bee lik a cuckwold.* Of course, as the carpenter is so newly married his fear would be accentuated. Although we are told that the carpenter loved Alison *moore than his lyf,* we are also shown that John's love is possessive, rather than liberating. Alison is kept *narwe in cage,/ For she was wild and yong.* Here Alison is being treated like a young, wild animal, to be caged in case she strays. Her age is mentioned deliberately so that the contrast in husband and wife's ages is emphasized. All that we hear about John is that he is 'old'.

The rest of the description relates his treatment of her rather than a full character description like that of Nicholas and Alison – and later Absolon. We are told that John has to *endure* his marriage to this young, lively girl who is obviously difficult to control in as much as he must try to protect what he considers is his.

Alison is described in great detail, as if she was a heroine from the courtly love tradition (see 'Romances and courtly love', p. 21). However, she is no noble lady, and the rural images which are used to describe her serve to remind us of this. For instance, no romantic heroine from a tale of courtly love would have a voice redolent of a chattering swallow, neither would she be referred to as a *popelote*, *primerole* or *piggesnie*, loosely translated as a 'poppet', 'primrose', or 'pretty thing' (the repeated plosive 'p' sounds suggest excitement). No courtly lover would describe a noble lady in such openly sexual terms – for example Alison's thighs are mentioned – and although she is described as making a good wife for a yeoman, she is apparently only good enough to be a lord's mistress. Alison is merely a very pretty and desirable country girl, who tries to make the most of herself by wearing the best clothes she can as she wants to look fashionable and expensive. We are left to wonder whether this is why she needs a rich husband! Her apron, however, reminds us that she is actually a working wife.

Her sexuality is emphasized through Chaucer's use of detailed description. For instance, the effect of the silk cloth suggests the outline of her body underneath, as does the reference to her girdle. Her shapely legs are hinted at by a description of her high-lacing boots, and her gored apron would no doubt set off her slim waist. She also conforms to the medieval ideal of beauty, having a fine forehead and plucked, curved eyebrows which frame her sexy, or *likerous* eyes. In this way Chaucer presents us with a comic parody of courtly love tales as seen through the eyes of the Miller.

Chaucer uses images of black and white to describe Alison. Her clothes are white with black embroidery, and her collar is made from black silk. Her hair and eyes are described as black as sloes, set off by her clothes, and her complexion is as bright and shining as a coin, which *in the Tour the noble yforged newe,* but the image also suggests mercantile value and brashness. Being a country wench, she is described in terms of the animals and healthy freshness of the countryside (see 'Imagery', p. 47). The vitality of the animals chosen to describe her also reflect her liveliness. Her apron is described as *white as morne milk,* and her prettiness is compared to the blossom on a pear tree, or a primrose. Her breath is compared with the sweetness of mead, ale and honey, or a hoard of hidden apples which have been stored in hay or heather, just waiting to be enjoyed: *Hir mouth was sweete as bragot or the meeth,/ Or hoord of apples leyd in hey or heeth.* Note that the senses of taste and smell are mentioned in the imagery used. Smell and taste are also mentioned in connection with Nicholas, who spreads fragrant herbs around his room, and later in connection with Absolon.

Although Alison's description gives the impression of freshness and sweetness, rather like Nicholas, her outward appearance hides the vulgar, coarse nature within. Chaucer may well have chosen images of black and white to represent the two sides of Alison's personality. ✪ How does Chaucer prepare the audience for Alison's subsequent seduction in this passage?

Section 3

Lines 163, *Now sire, and eft, sire, so bifel the cas,* to 198, *And pleyeth faste, and maketh melodie.*

◆ Nicholas makes a pass at Alison.
◆ A plan is hatched to fool the carpenter.

CAUGHT BY THE CROTCH!

We are told that on one occasion when the carpenter was at Osney, the crafty, obliging Nicholas, burning with desire for Alison, made a pass at her, grabbing her by the crotch and begging her to sleep with him. He declares he will die if she turns him down! Despite Alison's struggles, she cannot break free from his clutches, and so threatens to call for help unless he lets her go. However, Nicholas is persuasive and much more attractive than John, so she does not need much persuading. ✪ Why does Alison struggle but not call for help?

LET'S PLAY IT COOL BEFORE WE FOOL

Alison tells Nicholas that her husband is so jealous that if he finds out she may as well be dead, so they must act discreetly. Nicholas is confident that someone of his learning can easily fool a mere carpenter. He eagerly looks forward to his amorous liaison, slaps Alison's backside, kisses her, picks up his dulcimer and begins to play.

STYLE AND LANGUAGE

Nicholas's coarse way of wooing, and Alison's initial response to him, are a parody of courtly love, and contrast sharply with the behaviour of the courtly lover. He is referred to as *ful subtil and ful queynte*. *Subtil* can either mean subtle or artful, and Nicholas is certainly not thinking about being subtle towards Alison. For instance, his ability to *spak so faire* to Alison at the same time as groping her private parts is rather incongruous! Alison herself is not exactly unwilling, and her objections do not last very long. She could have yelled for help at any time, had she really wanted to. Her appearance of virtue is a sham.

It is ironic that when she finally does agree to become Nicholas's lover she feels the need to swear to him using the name of a holy saint, Thomas of Kent (Thomas à Becket). There is further irony in that this is the very shrine that the company of pilgrims are visiting. As a further parody of the courtly love genre, and as another example of Chaucer's irony, Nicholas is once more referred to as *hende* which could now be taken to mean 'obliging', or 'on the scene'. ❂ The conflict between the clerk and the carpenter can be said to have begun in this passage. What words and phrases show this conflict?

Section 4

Lines 199, *Thanne fil it thus, that to the parissh chirche,* to line 243, *For curteisie, he seide, he wolde noon.*

◆ We are introduced to Absolon.
◆ Absolon's amorous nature.

A FINE FOP

Alison makes a trip to her parish church one saint's day. She finishes her work and scrubs her forehead so that it is clean and shining. Absolon is parish clerk. He has curly yellow hair which falls over his shoulders, a rosy complexion and grey eyes. His clothing was also as pretty as a picture. His shoes are decorated to look like St Paul's church window, and he wears a smart red hose, an elegant light blue tunic and a fine white surplice. Some of his duties include being the local barber and blood-letter, and he also draws up land charters. He is fond of merrymaking and dancing he is an accomplished musician. He plays a small two-stringed fiddle and the guitar, and sings in a high voice. He entertains everyone in the brewhouses and taverns in the town, concentrating especially on those inns with pretty barmaids. He is very fussy about how he speaks, and has a particular squeamishness about farting! ✪ Do you find anything comical about Absolon in this passage? What?

GOLDEN CURLS AND AN EYE FOR THE GIRLS

We are told that on holy days Absolon's duties would involve swinging the censer in church. He uses these occasions to eye up the women in the pews. On this particular day his amorous gaze falls on Alison. He immediately becomes infatuated to such an extent that he refuses, out of courtesy, to take any of the wives' offerings of money at the service. ✪ Does refusing the women's money say anything about Absolon's character?

✎ STYLE AND LANGUAGE

Absolon is described as a very effeminate man (see 'Characterization', p. 31). Chaucer creates an amusing picture of this particular 'dandy', who flings his legs flamboyantly about in twenty manere when he dances, and who goes round the Oxford taverns eyeing up the barmaids and crooning to them in a loud quinible, always immaculately turned out. He has a particular love of showy clothes and chooses to wear bright red or blue. Even his shoes are a talking point. Absolon apes the behaviour and manners of the courtly lover, playing his guitar and – unlike Nicholas – making sure he gets heard by traipsing round the local hostelries. By introducing Absolon's particular weakness, *he was somdeel squaymous/ Of farting*, immediately after references to his musical abilities makes for a wonderful comic contrast, and prepares the audience for the subsequent events of the Tale.

Notice how animal imagery is used to describe Absolon . His eyes are *grey as goos,* and his predatory feelings towards Alison when he sees her are described in terms of a hunting cat: *I dar wel seyn if she hadde been a mous,/ And he a cat, he wolde hire hente anon.* For all his courtly pretensions, Absolon has his own darker side of animal lust. In addition, notice how Absolon turns a devotional practice such as the swinging of a censer into a sexual overture, and uses his duties in church to eye up the women there. He also tries to impress them: *That of no wyf took he noon offringe.* However, by refusing money he is not helping the Church, but gratifying his own ego.

Alison prepares herself before she visits the church as she wants to look her best. She scrubs her grimy forehead until it is glowing, indicating that she must have been used to dirty physical work. The audience is again reminded of her status as a carpenter's wife, as opposed to a noble lady.

Section 5

Lines 244, *The moone, whan it was night, ful brighte shoon,* to 290, *For Absolon may waille and singe 'allas'.*

◆ Absolon tries unsuccessfully to woo Alison.

ABSOLON THE ABSOLUTE ASS

Absolon courts Alison at night by playing his guitar under her bedroom window, asking her to take pity on him, just as if he was a real 'courtly lover'. However, the foppish Absolon and the pretty, skittish carpenter's wife are no noble lord and lady caught in a love triangle. Absolon's crooning wakes John, but his courtship continues nevertheless. He combs his hair, spruces himself up and enlists people to act as go-betweens in the courtship. He sends her gifts of spiced wine, ale, mead, and little cakes hot from the oven. As she lives in town he offers her money which she can spend easily. He even tries to impress her by taking the part of Herod in the Mystery Play, a role completely unsuited to his high, quavering voice. All this is to no avail, however, as Alison continues her affair with Nicholas. This, says the Miller, proves the old maxim that the person on the spot always wins over the distant lover.

 STYLE AND LANGUAGE

Notice how the night is described as being ideal for the courtly lover, *The moon ... shone*, and Absolon is determined to abide by chivalric clichés. However, the absurdity of Absolon's postures in the moonlight have their comic contrast in the stark realism of Alison's and John's reactions inside the bedroom.

The Miller's Tale contains many wise sayings. There is much truth in the proverb *Alwey the nie slie maketh the ferre leeve to be looth* as it is the lodger, Nicholas, who actually lives in the same house as Alison and who has the advantage over Absolon. Although the narrator mentions that Alison *loveth so this hende Nicholas*, we might well question the reference to 'love' here, as Alison is motivated by lust every bit as much as the rival lovers.

Notice how general points on courtship are expressed, one after the other: *For som folk wol ben wonnen for richesse,/ And somme for strokes, and somme for gentillesse.* Absolon's attempts to woo Alison fail, and even gifts of alcohol cannot make her feel romantically inclined! Absolon's determination then extends to gifts of money, which suggests that Alison has monetary value: *And, for she was of the town, he profred meede.* ✪ Why does Chaucer mention the height of Alison's bedroom window? Which words and phrases in this passage highlight Absolon's absurdity?

Section 6

Lines 290, *And so bifel it on a Saterday,* to 339, *In what array he saugh this ilke man.*

◆ Nicholas devises a scheme.
◆ Nicholas hides in his room.

CRAFTY NICK DEVISES A TRICK

One Saturday, when the carpenter is away in Osney on business, Nicholas devises a scheme to deceive the jealous John which would enable them to spend the night together. This scheme involves Nicholas taking enough food and drink to last for a day or two into his room, where he will stay. If the carpenter enquires as to his whereabouts, Alison is told to say that she has not seen him all day and is worried about his health, as her maid has also heard nothing in response to her calls. ❂ Why do you think Alison and Nicholas do not take advantage of the carpenter's absence?

JOHN'S FEARS GROW AS NICK LIES LOW

On Saturday Nicholas remains quietly hidden in his room, eating and sleeping until the following Sunday evening. The carpenter, puzzled by his absence, wonders if there is anything wrong, swearing by St Thomas that all is not well. Perhaps Nicholas is ill and might die? After all, it is an insecure world, and John has, that very Monday, seen the corpse of a man taken for burial who the previous day had been in excellent health. With these fears in mind, John tells his serving man to go to Nicholas's door and call him, bang on it with a stone, and then let the anxious carpenter know what is going on. This boy does, calling to Nicholas and asking him why he appears to be sleeping so long. As he receives no reply he peers through the cat-hole in the wooden boards and sees Nicholas staring into space as if he is moonstruck. He rushes downstairs to tell his master what he has seen. ❂ Does the carpenter express genuine fears about Nicholas's welfare?

STYLE AND LANGUAGE

Chaucer is specific about marking definite periods of time. The trick is 'hatched' on a Saturday when John is away and put into practice over a weekend, Nicholas remaining in his room until Sunday evening. The imaginary Flood is scheduled for *a Monday next, at quarter night,* and the waters are due to subside *Aboute prime upon the nexte day.* This will give Alison and Nicholas a long time in bed together. It may seem ironic that Nicholas goes to great lengths to devise such an elaborate plot when John is often absent, but perhaps we should remember that Nicholas is spurred on by his desire to outwit the carpenter with his intellectual superiority and the plot is therefore part of Nicholas's ego trip.

Nicholas pretends to be petrified by his revelation, staring upwards *As he hadde kikked on the newe moone,* as the popular belief was that staring at the moon brought on madness, or 'lunacy' (which comes from *luna* – the moon). The servant discovers this by peering through a hole in the wall. Much of this Tale seems to involve characters knocking on doors and windows, wondering what is going on inside locked rooms!

Notice John's fondness of philosophical clichés which ironically rebound on himself. An example in this passage is: *This world is now ful tikel, sikerly.* In fact, John's world will certainly become unstable, both metaphorically and literally, later in the Tale!

Section 7

Lines 340, *This carpenter to blessen him began,* to 387, *I wol telle it noon oother man, certein.*

◆ The carpenter blames Nicholas's 'affliction' on his study of astrology.
◆ John confronts Nicholas.

SPACED OUT, SEEING STARS

The carpenter asks the patron saint of Oxford, St Frideswide, for help. He believes that his lodger has been meddling with too many divine secrets in his studies of *astromie* and so has been punished with madness. Ignorant men are blessed, he says, for *Men sholde nat knowe of Goddes privetee.* He recalls how he knew of another such student who was so obsessed with astrological predictions that he failed to see the clay-pit he was walking towards! He then resolves to upbraid Nicholas for his studying and asks for his servant to bring a staff so that he can break down Nicholas's door. ✪ What is ironic about the carpenter's reflections in this passage?

JOHN WEAVES SPELLS; NICK FORETELLS

John and his servant dislodge Nicholas's door from its hinges and enter his room, only to see Nicholas sitting as still as a stone, gazing upwards into space. The carpenter shakes him and asks him to pray to be kept free from divine punishment. John then rushes round to all four corners of his house reciting a spell to keep away the evil eye. Eventually Nicholas 'comes to', mutters something about a disaster coming to the world and asks for a drink, telling the carpenter that he wants to tell him a secret.

STYLE AND LANGUAGE

In this passage John ironically sets himself up as Nicholas's superior in that being an ignorant man he does not spy into God's secrets. This comes across as yet another of John's somewhat bombastic, and ironic, sayings:

> *I thoghte ay wel how that it sholde be!*
> *Men sholde nat knowe of Goddes privetee.*
> *Ye, blessed be alwey a lewed man*
> *That noght but oonly his bileve kan!*

In addition, John reveals a certain amount of self-satisfaction in recalling that another academic was so preoccupied with his study that he accidentally fell into a clay-pit. Here John's inverted snobbery reveals itself.

Notice how Nicholas's immobility, *sat ay as stille as stoon,* contrasts dramatically with John's frantic activity: *Get me a staf, that I may underspore,/ Whil that thou, Robin, hevest up the dore.* John also rushes around weaving spells while

Nicholas remains still, in charge of the situation. These night spells show the carpenter's superstitious nature and his gullibility, of which Nicholas is able to take full advantage.

Section 8

Lines 388, *This carpenter goth doon, and comth agein*, to 492, *Go, save oure lyf, and that I the biseche*.

◆ Nicholas tells the carpenter about his 'revelation'.
◆ He talks of his 'escape plan'.
◆ The carpenter is sworn to secrecy.

THE ARTFUL ASTROLOGER

The carpenter rushes downstairs to fetch a large jug of ale for himself and the apparently shaken Nicholas. When he returns, he is sworn to secrecy as Nicholas relates his story of the fake Flood. If John repeats it to anybody, says Nicholas, he will be afflicted with madness, but John assures him that he is no tell-tale or gossip. Nicholas then says that through his astrological calculations and by staring at the moon, he has had it revealed to him that on the following Monday, at about nine o'clock in the evening, there will be such a downpour that the whole world will be overwhelmed in less than half an hour. The gullible carpenter is aghast, and is so distraught at the thought that Alison might be drowned, that he almost collapses. ❂ Why do you think that Nicholas chose to 'recover' from his trance the moment the carpenter had finished his white-magic spells? How does Nicholas build up the carpenter's credulity in this passage?

BUILD A BOAT SO YOU CAN FLOAT

Nicholas tells the carpenter that the only survivors will be himself, John and Alison. He then reminds John about the story of Noah, referring to the popular myth that Noah's wife made such a fuss about boarding the Ark, that she had to be put on a separate ship on her own. The carpenter is then told to make three boats from the tubs used for kneading dough or brewing beer. These makeshift 'boats' should be hung from the rafters and kept out of sight. John is told to put enough provisions for a day inside each of them as the waters would apparently subside by nine in the morning of the following day. John is also told to put an axe in each tub, which would be used to cut the rope tying the boats to the ceiling when the water, supposedly, reaches roof-height.

❂ Do we sympathize with John at any point in this passage?

SILENCE, SECRECY, AND NO SEX!

John is warned not to tell his servant Robin or his maid Gill, using the excuse that they cannot be 'saved'. Nicholas then paints an attractive picture of how John and Nicholas will be rulers of the earth after the Flood. He is careful to remind John that the three of them should be absolutely silent from the time that they get into their tubs on the following night until they are 'delivered'. In addition, says Nicholas, it is important that John and Alison must abstain from sex during that time, for reasons of 'purity'. Nicholas bids farewell to John, flattering his vanity by saying *Thou art so wys, it needeth thee nat teche.*

STYLE AND LANGUAGE

Nicholas delays telling John about the Flood until after the carpenter has gone downstairs, has returned with plenty of ale, and has been sworn to secrecy. This creates more dramatic tension and ensures that the carpenter is fully aware of the importance of secrecy. Both silence and lack of sex are, of course, imperative for Nicholas's plan to spend the night with Alison himself! Notice also how the 'Flood waters' will last until the lovers have had time to spend the night together.

The carpenter shows his lack of knowledge as he is apparently unaware that God promises Noah in the Bible that there would never be another Flood. In addition, Nicholas reminds John of the fictitious version of the Flood which is shown in the popular Mystery Plays, where Noah's wife is made out to be a scold who refuses to board the Ark. This episode is there simply to create comedy, and has no biblical foundation. This version is told to the carpenter as it prepares the way for Nicholas to mention that they should have a 'boat' each, vital for his sexual liaison with Alison. Nicholas is prepared even to blaspheme in order to achieve his end, claiming that he is speaking the words of God: *For it is Cristes conseil that I seye.* Notice the irony behind Nicholas's statement *I wol nat tellen Goddes privetee*, as obviously Nicholas has already told John a good many of the Almighty's 'secrets'!

An additional tactic Nicholas uses here is to prey upon John's vanity, which he does by painting a picture of himself and the carpenter being *lordes al oure lyf/ Of al the world*, and also by referring to John's apparent wisdom, using a proverb for further conviction: *Men seyn thus, 'Sende the wise, and sey no thing'.* Of course Nicholas knows perfectly well that the carpenter is far from *wys*, and he capitalizes – and no doubt revels – in the extent of John's ignorance. Nicholas uses another proverb to impress John later in his diatribe, which he attributes to Solomon: *Werk al by conseil, and thou shalt nat rewe.* The carpenter would also be taken in by the wily student's appealing reference to the *white doke* swimming after *hire drake*, an image of Alison's wifely submissiveness and devotion.

Nicholas is a wonderful salesman and con artist. He knows just how to prey upon John's fears, and how to make him feel special, apparently being made privy to some important information. John is referred to as Nicholas's *lief and deere* landlord, and he makes him swear a solemn oath of secrecy *upon thy trouthe* which John, with his love of superstition and ritual, would take extremely seriously. Nicholas does not tell John his 'news' straight away, but builds on John's credulity and awe by using words such as *Cristes conseil, forlore* and *vengeaunce.* Naturally John would not question Nicholas's learning, leaving the way open for Nicholas to fool John with references to astrological studies and biblical references. As already mentioned, John's biblical knowledge is sketchy, so Nicholas can mention Solomon and Noah to his heart's content, except that the stories John probably knows best may well have been the adaptations of the Mystery Plays (see 'Literary background', p. 20).

Nicholas carefully uses persuasive language, such as the repetition of the phrase *hastow nat herd*, when discussing the Bible. John would be very unlikely to admit his ignorance to his own lodger, even if he is a learned student. Of course, this sort of ruse will only work if the recipient of the lie is ignorant and vain, as John is! At no time does John ever stop to wonder why he, his wife and his lodger are apparently singled out for divine salvation, and why he should be chosen to be joint ruler of the earth with Nicholas after the Flood.

Nicholas's plans are made to seem plausible when he uses nautical terms, such as *mast and seil, shipe, barge,* and *shippes bord.* This is all the more comical because these 'ships' are to be created from kneading troughs or *kymelins.* Chaucer has to be careful to make Nicholas's story seem plausible to the credulous carpenter but ridiculous to the townsfolk who consider John to be mad for believing in a second Flood!

Test yourself

> **?** Nicholas and Absolon are rivals for Alison's affections, but they are very different types in many ways. Mind Map their similarities and differences.
> **?** Imagine that John has written to an agony column about his problems. Write his letter, and the reply he receives.

Section 9

Lines 493, *This sely carpenter goth forth his wey,* to 548, *And freres in the chauncel gonne singe.*

◆ The carpenter tells Alison about the Flood.
◆ He makes preparations.
◆ They climb into their boats.
◆ Alison and Nicholas slip off when the carpenter is asleep.

A DUBIOUS DELUGE

John tells Alison about the coming 'Flood'. She puts on a good act of expressing fear and concern, begging him to do something to save them, even going so far as to remind him of her loyalty, referring to herself as *thy true, verray wedded wyf.*

THREE TRUSTY TUBS

In secret, the carpenter makes clumsy attempts at constructing three 'boats' and hangs them from the roof beams, filling them with enough bread, cheese and ale to last for a day. In addition, he constructs three rustic ladders so that the boats can be boarded by himself, Alison and Nicholas. He then sends his serving man and his maid to London on a pretend errand.

CARPENTER CUCKOLDED AT CURFEW

When the fateful Monday arrives, John makes sure everything is prepared. He extinguishes his candles, they climb into their boats, remind each other to keep *clom*, and sit in silence for a few minutes. John says his prayers and waits for the rain. Eventually he falls asleep from stress and exhaustion. He begins to snore as his head is lying in an awkward position. Nicholas and Alison then quietly creep back down their ladders and jump into bed together, delighting in their lovemaking until the bell summons the monks to go to chapel to sing *laudes*, or praises to God.

STYLE AND LANGUAGE

Note how the Miller uncharacteristically steps outside the story to comment on the action. He comments upon the power of the imagination and the way it affects the carpenter in three lines of philosophical rhetoric – possibly unusual for a drunken Miller:

> *Lo which a greet thing is affeccioun!*
> *Men may dyen of imaginacioun,*
> *So depe may impressioun be take.*

In other words, 'men die several times before their deaths'. If John has little in the way of intellect, then his fanciful nature certainly makes up for the deficiency!

There are many examples of verbs used in this passage which accentuate the frantic activity of the carpenter as he makes his speedy preparations for the impending flood, such as: *wepeth, waileth, siketh, gooth, getteth, heng, made, vitailled, sende, shette, dressed, clomben.* John's efforts only serve to make him more ridiculous to the audience, as we know about the ruse.

The clumsiness and homespun nature of John's preparations emphasizes the farcical nature of the whole affair, for instance: the placing of the simple fare – bread, cheese and good ale – in the tubs; the secret construction of home-made ladders which can be climbed by *the ronges and the stalkes* to reach boats made from *kneding troghs* and *kymelins;* the shutting of the carpenter's door and the blowing out of the candles; the reference to sitting in the 'boats' for as long as it takes to walk *a furlong way.* These all serve to stress the ridiculous nature of the situation and John's rustic ignorance.

Notice how the passage contains some notable examples of irony. For example, Alison's protestations of loyalty, *I am thy trewe, verray wedded wyf,* when she is obviously far from faithful, and the incongruous mixture of sex and religion with the mention of the monks' bells. There is also irony in the picture which we are given of the snoring carpenter, squashed into his absurd tub tied to the rafters – more of a figure of fun from the Mystery Plays than a potential postdiluvian ruler of the world.

The stealthy way in which Alison and Nicholas creep down the ladder in almost indecent haste is rather distasteful: *Doun of the laddre stalketh Nicholay,/ And Alisoun ful softe adoun she spedde.* ✪ The Miller skims over the activities of Nicholas and Alison in bed, when elsewhere in the Tale we are treated to bawdy detail. Why do you think the 'bed scene' is left out?

Section 10

Line 549, *This parissh clerk, this amorous Absolon,* to 578, *And al the night thanne wol I wake and pleye.*

◆ Absolon learns of the carpenter's 'absence'.
◆ Absolon decides to declare his love.

WHEN THE CARPENTER'S AWAY ...

The lovelorn Absolon, spending that same Monday in Osney, asks a monk if he has seen the carpenter recently. The monk takes him quietly aside and says that John has not been seen since Saturday, when he was sent by the abbot to get timber. The monk says that John is either staying at a distant farmstead for a day or so, or else he must be at his home. He assures Absolon that he cannot say definitely where John is. ❂ How is Absolon's devious nature exposed here?

... THE CLERK WILL PLAY

Absolon's spirits lift on hearing the news of John's apparent disappearance. Surely, thinks Absolon, the time has now come to declare his love once more for Alison. He decides to creep to her bedroom window during the night and beg a kiss. He has also received signs which he believes means his luck will change. For instance, his mouth has itched all day and he has dreamed of a feast – sure signs of sexual success! Absolon decides to get some rest before his amorous adventure.

STYLE AND LANGUAGE

We are quickly reminded of Absolon's predominant characteristic, *That is for love alwey so wo bigon.* However, Absolon is not so 'romantic' that he cannot check on the carpenter's whereabouts before he calls on Alison.

Notice how Chaucer shifts perspective to show what Absolon has been up to earlier, rather as the contemporary film-maker uses 'flashbacks'. Absolon's juvenile approach to courtship is shown by the use of the word *pleye* which can be used to mean 'entertainment', as well as lovemaking. As the monk who talks to Absolon takes him aside to give him the information about John, presumably he knows of his infatuation with Alison. Absolon's light-hearted excitement at the prospect of wooing Alison is stressed: *This Absolon ful joly was and light.* This highlights his forthcoming humiliation.

Absolon has joined the ranks of those who can predict the future with his superstitious beliefs that having an itchy mouth means a kiss, and dreaming of a feast means sexual gratification. The irony is of course, that Absolon *does* eventually get to kiss Alison, and to have a 'feast', but neither will prove much to his taste! Absolon's itching mouth will also feature later in the Tale when he desperately tries to clean his lips. The fact that Absolon mentions that he will knock on Alison's window *at cockkes crowe* is a parody of the courtly love ritual.

Section 11

Lines 579, *Whan that the first cok hath crowe, anon,* to 616, *'Now hust, and thou shalt laughen al thy fille.'*

◆ Absolon spruces himself up for to pay a courtship visit.
◆ He croons to Alison outside her window.
◆ Absolon gets a sharp reply, and begs a kiss.

SWEET NOTHINGS ...

Like the fop he is, Absolon preens himself for his nocturnal visit. He dresses in his best clothes, combs his hair, and takes great care to ensure his breath smells sweet. He croons at Alison's bedroom window, not knowing that she is with Nicholas, referring to her as *hony-comb, faire brid* and *sweet cinamome*, declaring that he has broken out in a sweat for her love and has lost his appetite. ✪ Is anything ironic about Absolon's scrupulous preparations?

... SOUR REPLIES

Alison's irritated reply, telling him that he is a 'Jack fool' who is out of luck as far as she is concerned, is in sharp contrast with the wooing of the amorous Absolon, who fancies himself as the romantic lover! Alison shows her contempt by starkly stating that she loves someone else *wel bet than thee.* She even threatens to throw a stone at him if he does not go away and let her sleep (having tired herself out with lovemaking). Absolon's childish whining in the hope of gaining her sympathy has backfired. His plaintive, submissive *ye certes lemman* in reply to her scornful words is the catalyst for her plan to make a fool of Absolon. ✪ What do we learn about Alison in this section?

✎ STYLE AND LANGUAGE

Absolon's preparations for courtship are described in detail, showing him up to be an effeminate dandy. He grooms himself *at point devis*, from top to toe, combing his hair and dressing in fine clothes. He pays a great deal of attention to oral hygiene, chewing cardamom and liquorice, and putting a leaf of herb paris under his tongue for good luck. (Absolon's revulsion for bad smells and tastes becomes very significant later!) Many of the images in this passage are ironically connected with smell or taste, for example *hony-comb, sweete Alison, sweete cinamome* – epithets which Absolon withdraws after his 'kiss'! Absolon also uses images connected with animals and birds, such as a lamb or turtle dove. However, his attempts at gaining Alison's sympathy only succeed in making him look pathetic. For instance, he describes how he pines for her like *a lamb after the tete*, which makes him appear childish.

Absolon only accentuates his effeminacy in Alison's eyes when he mentions that he has lost his appetite, and *may nat ete na moore than a maide*. Of course, 'real men' such as Nicholas, enjoy their food! (It should be remembered that Nicholas asks for sufficient food to be sent to his room during the time of his 'disappearance', as well as reminding John to put enough food in the boats to last out the 'Flood'.)

In comic contrast with what Absolon believes to be irresistible, tender wooings, are Alison's blunt, coarse replies: Absolon is a *Jakke fool* who should *go forth thy way* in the name of *twenty devel*, unless he wants a stone thrown at him. Alison's mention of *I love another – and elles I were to blame –/ Wel bet than thee* is ambiguous in that it could be Alison insulting Absolon's sexual prowess, as well as meaning that she simply prefers someone else.

Section 12

Lines 615, *This Absolon doun sette him on his knees,* to 651, *And weep as dooth a child that is ybete.*

◆ Absolon gets an unexpected shock.
◆ He is cured of romantic love and wants revenge.

KISSES ON THE BOTTOM

Absolon gets down on his knees in front of the window saying that he is a gentleman behaving in a gentlemanly way, simply hoping for future rewards. He calls on Alison, asking her to favour him with the promised kiss. She opens the window quickly, attributing her haste to her fear of neighbours seeing what was happening. Absolon wipes his lips dry, preparing for his wonderful kiss, while Alison sticks her bare backside out of the window. It takes Absolon a few minutes before he realizes that what he is kissing with such ardour is rough and hairy. 'Surely a woman hasn't got a beard,' Absolon muses to himself. Suddenly the awful truth hits him. He starts back disgusted, while Alison turns around and slams the window shut with a titter. ✪ Is Absolon's thought that *a womman hath no berd* unnecessarily graphic detail or is it included to highlight Absolon's humiliation?

FROM ROMANCE TO REVENGE

Absolon is mortified and livid with anger as he listens to Nicholas's glee at the success of the joke. He declares that he would rather have revenge for his humiliation than to own the whole town of Oxford! He scrubs his lips furiously with dust, sand, straw, cloth and woodchips – anything to get them clean again! He curses his lack of foresight. Since kissing Alison's bare backside, he has been cured of his infatuation. Denouncing all love affairs, he takes himself off, weeping like a child who has been smacked. ✪ Why is Absolon's attitude to future love-affairs mentioned here?

STYLE AND LANGUAGE

This passage is ironic because it shows the build up of Absolon's hopes still further. He sets himself on his knees in a subservient position awaiting his kiss, the positioning of the low window being very important for subsequent events. His wish, *For after this I hope ther cometh moore*, is also ironic. The action of wiping his lips, and the relish with which he kisses, *he kiste her naked ers / Ful savourly*, is emphasized so that his mistake will seem all the more revolting to him.

Alison cunningly hurries Absolon so he will not realize what is happening. She does this by mentioning the need for haste because of the neighbours, *lest that oure neighebores thee espie*, in spite of the fact that it is doubtful that anybody would have seen anything, since *Derk was the night as pich, or as the cole*. However, Alison has revealed herself to be as quick-witted and sly as the *wezele* with which she is compared earlier. Absolon considers that he has behaved impeccably, like a lord courting his lady. The expressions he uses, *thy grace* and *thyn oore*, are conventional phrases taken from the language of courtly love. This contrasts comically with Alison's earthy, *Have do, com of, and speed the faste*, which exposes Absolon's lovesick posturing as nonsense.

Notice how the frenzied way in which Absolon tries to clean his mouth after 'kissing' contrasts ironically with the elaborate preparations he makes earlier: *Who rubbeth now, who froteth now his lippes/ With dust, with sond, with straw, with clooth, with chippes.* Chaucer's initial apology for the vulgarity of the Miller's story is seen as very necessary in this passage, as both the expre: *berd* can also mean 'a joke', and no doubt the coarse Miller had in mind the sexual overtones of *queynte* in the line *His hoote love was coold and al yqueynt.* The fact that Absolon hears Nicholas's cry of delight, *A berd! a berd!*, means that Absolon will be even keener to get his revenge. Absolon's humiliation comes across to the audience as being total, as we are told that the misplaced kiss incident affects all his future relationships, and every time he remembers he weeps *as dooth a childe that is ybete.*

Section 13

Lines 652, *A softe paas he wente over the strete,* to 689, *This wol I yeve thee, if thou me kisse.*

◆ Absolon visits Gervase the blacksmith.
◆ Absolon returns for his revenge.

HOT FOR REVENGE

Absolon, determined to get his revenge, visits Gervase the blacksmith, who is surprised to see him so early in the morning. Noticing Absolon's agitated state, Gervase assumes that Absolon is in the throes of sexual excitement and teases him with suggestive references to women, which backfire completely as Absolon is certainly not in the mood! Absolon persuades Gervase to lend him a red-hot coulter, part of a ploughshare he was making. ❍ What effect does Absolon's silence have on the reader in this section?

THE BURNING BRAND

Absolon quietly returns to the carpenter's window, coughs and knocks. Alison angrily yells at the 'thief' to go away. Absolon tells her that he has brought her a fine gold ring, beautifully decorated, which his mother has given to him. He says that if she gives him a kiss it would be hers. He has decided that his revenge will be sweet. ○ Why does Absolon cough and then knock at the window?

✍ STYLE AND LANGUAGE

Notice how everything is done 'quietly' – crossing the street, knocking on Gervase's door – which serves to emphasize the secrecy, tricks and double-tricks that are going on between the characters in so much of this Tale.

Absolon's hot, lustful passion has been transformed to cold cunning in the way in which he goes about making plans for his revenge. He has not let on that he has realized what has happened to him, and he is obviously aware of Alison's acquisitive nature. Chaucer builds up the suspense of the scene very skilfully. Absolon *cogheth*, then knocks gently at Alison's window before laying his trap. It is almost possible to hear the bile in Absolon's wheedlingly persuasive *sweete leef* and *deerling*, before going on to mention the non-existent ring; he is an excellent salesman. However, the audience knows he desires revenge, and his words, albeit romantic (which they would need to be to fool Alison and Nicholas), take on sinister overtones.

Notice Gervase's use of colloquial expressions when he greets Absolon: *What, Absolon! for Cristes sweete tree*; *benedictee;* and *By Seinte Note.* Not only is he genuinely surprised to see Absolon out and about so early, but this language also reveals Gervase's bluff friendliness, giving the impression that he is as open and generous with his property as he is with the language he uses, *Certes, were it gold,/ Or in a poke nobles alle untold,/ Thou sholdest have, as I am trewe smith*, unless of course Absolon's urgency is provoking sarcasm from Gervase! However, Absolon's blunt reply, refusing to tell Gervase why he wants the coulter, *therof be as be may*, shows just how seriously Absolon takes his humiliation. Notice Chaucer's use of homely, rustic expressions, such as *He hadde more tow on his distaf/ Than Gerveys knew*, taken from spinning, which describe Absolon's vengeful state of mind.

Section 14

Lines 690, *This Nicholas was risen for to pisse,* to 715, *Upon the floor, and ther aswowne he lay.*

◆ Nicholas is branded on the bottom.
◆ The carpenter falls to the floor in his tub.

RUMP STAKE

Nicholas, who has got up to relieve himself, thinks it is time for him to have some fun, and decides to put the finishing touches on the joke by getting Absolon to kiss his bare backside also. He opens the window and puts his rump out as far as his hips. In the meantime, Absolon, wanting to make exactly sure of the whereabouts of his target, asks 'Alison' to make a noise. Nicholas obligingly breaks wind in Absolon's face so noisily that it sounds like a thunderclap. Absolon then strikes Nicholas with the red-hot ploughshare right in the middle of his backside so that he has a burn the size of a hand. Nicholas is in so much agony he thinks he will die, and yells for water. ✪ Are you appalled or gratified by Nicholas's punishment?

A RUDE AWAKENING

On hearing the commotion and the shout, *water!* the carpenter wakes up with a start, believing that the great Flood has come. He takes his axe, cuts the rope tying his boat to the ceiling and falls to the floor like a stone, knocking himself out. ✪ The carpenter's reaction has been called a brilliant device. Why is this?

STYLE AND LANGUAGE

The fact that Nicholas had *risen for to pisse* shows the cruder side of this rather unromantic liaison. Nicholas's positioning of his rear end is important, *over the buttock to the haunche-bon,* as this will lend comic impact to what happens next. The wheedle from Absolon *'Spek, sweete brid, I noot nat where thou art'* and the beautifully timed loud flatulence is comic irony at its best. Of course, Nicholas has now given Absolon a vital clue to his whereabouts, which brings about Nicholas's own painful downfall! Here, Nicholas, always wanting to go one better, has brought about his own punishment.

The fast pace of this passage is well suited to the farcical nature of the events in which many pretensions of the characters are exposed. Nicholas's *let fle a fart* is a crude but effective way of shattering Absolon's romantic allusions. Similarly Nicholas's pride in outwitting both the carpenter and a disappointed sexual rival is also punished. The reference to *Nowelis flood* reveals the carpenter's ignorance as 'Noel' (meaning Christmas) is confused with 'Noah'. In addition, the language Chaucer uses is similarly appropriate to the occasion. For example the noise of Nicholas's fart is described as being *a thonder-dent*, appropriate for the coming of a 'Flood' ! ✪ Are we supposed to be appalled at the extent of Nicholas's injuries or pleased that he has received a 'just' punishment?

Section 15

Lines 714, *Up stirte hire Alison and Nicholay*, to 747, *Heere endeth the Millere his tale*.

◆ The carpenter is thought to be mad.
◆ The Tale is concluded.

THE TALE OF THREE TUBS

Alison and Nicholas raise the alarm, and tell the curious neighbours that the carpenter has had delusions of *Nowelis flood* coming to destroy the world. Every time John tries to speak to clear his name, he is talked down by Alison and Nicholas. The townsfolk find it all highly amusing and peer up into the roof to see the two remaining boats hanging there, joking about John's suffering, despite the fact that he has a broken arm. From that day on John is considered mad throughout Oxford, and all the students take Nicholas's side. ✪ Do you feel any sympathy for John?

A CHUCKLING CONCLUSION

In this way the jealous carpenter finds himself cuckolded in spite of his possessiveness, Absolon feels humiliated because he has kissed Alison's 'nether regions' and Nicholas is branded on the bottom. The Miller finishes his Tale and asks for God's blessing on the company. ○ Why has Alison escaped punishment? Why has the Miller finished his story so abruptly?

STYLE AND LANGUAGE

Notice how the fast pace of the narrative is kept up to the end of the Tale by describing the neighbours who come rushing to see what has been happening: *The neighebores, both smale and grete,/ In ronnen for to gauren on this man.* Alison and Nicholas emphasize John's madness by repeating *Nowelis flood* when they tell the 'story' to the townsfolk. The public humiliation of John is stressed, and the verdict is unanimous, the townsfolk and students all firmly believe in John's madness – the former respected carpenter is now a social outcast: *He was holde wood in al the toun;/ For every clerk anonright heeld with oother.*

The Miller does not mince words as he sums up the consequences of the events of his bawdy Tale in a mere four lines, showing the characters getting their come-uppance because of their pride and folly.

CRITICAL APPROACHES

There are many different interpretations of *The Miller's Tale*. These critical approaches can be divided into a variety of groups. No one type of interpretation is 'right' or 'wrong'. However, by comparing various approaches you will be able to gain a broader perspective on the text.

Historicist approaches

Some critics believe that it is impossible to separate the text from the times in which it was written. They see the characters and events as being part and parcel of the huge political, social and economic changes which were taking place in the fourteenth century. These critics, or historicists as they are known, might consider that in order to understand the Miller, his Tale, and his characters it is necessary to know about contemporary attitudes, beliefs and opinions, and about the social and political structure of the fourteenth century. This might include looking at the economic position of millers or carpenters, or examining the roles of clerks. Well-known historicists include Professor Lee Patterson (*Negotiating the Past*, 1987), and Janette Dillon (*Geoffrey Chaucer*, 1993).

Marxist interpretations

These critics are interested in the power struggles between classes, and how this is reflected in the literature of the time. Marxist critics see Chaucer not as a representative male of the Middle Ages, but as a writer who opposed the dominant institutions of his day, such as the Church, and dominant cultural concepts such as the code of chivalry, while also adopting an unconventional view of the roles of men and women (D. Aers, *Chaucer, Langland and the creative imagination*, 1980). Although these institutions would be allowed a voice in his work, they would be undermined or subverted in some way. *The Miller's Tale* would be interpreted by such critics as attacking the established status quo. For instance, the rivalry between Nicholas, Absolon and the carpenter would be taken to represent common conflicts between the genteel class (Nicholas), yeoman class (John) and the Church (Absolon).

Dramatic interpretations

Some critics consider *The Miller's Tale* to be part of the larger group of Tales. These critics think that it is necessary to view each Tale and its teller as part of a larger whole, rather like the Acts in a play (for example, *The Miller's Tale* reflects *The Knight's Tale*, and *The Reeve's Tale* 'quits' *The Miller's Tale*). G. L. Kittredge suggests that the various tales should be seen as dramatic soliloquies by their fictional tellers, stating that the stories exist because of the pilgrims, and not the other way around. These stories he believes to be long speeches which reveal either directly, or more subtly, the characters of their narrators (*Chaucer and His Poetry*, 1915).

Deconstructionist criticism

The critics known as deconstructionists assume that the language of a text refers only to itself, and that the 'meaning' of a text bears only an accidental relationship to the author's intention. Such critics recognize that the words an author uses cannot always be used as precise clues to meaning, for somewhere else in the text the author's 'meaning' may seem entirely contradictory. A text can therefore be open to many, and possibly conflicting, interpretations. These critics find it difficult to decide on the precise meanings of the words that Chaucer uses, and so consider that this might account for the many complexities found in *The Miller's Tale* and other works by Chaucer. For example, H. Leicester says that the pilgrims do not create the texts that they speak on the road to Canterbury. Instead he believes that the texts, by virtue of being spoken, create the pilgrims (H. Leicester, *The Disenchanted Self*, 1990).

Feminist interpretations

Certain feminist critics investigate anti-feminism in the Tales. For example, the Knight's Emily, and the Miller's Alison can be seen as his definitive statements on courtly and bourgeois images of women (P. H. Weissman, *Anti-feminism and Chaucer's Characterization of Women*, 1975). It is debateable, however, how much Alison can be seen as 'passive', or the 'victim' of a male-dominated society. For instance, she seems to know her mind with regard to suitors, and she plays an active part in the humiliation of Absolon and the discrediting of John. It could be argued perhaps that, by taking a lover she was following the only course of action open to a woman in the fourteenth century trapped in an unsuitable marriage. On the other hand, it might be considered that Alison and her actions illustrated the medieval belief in the fickleness of women.

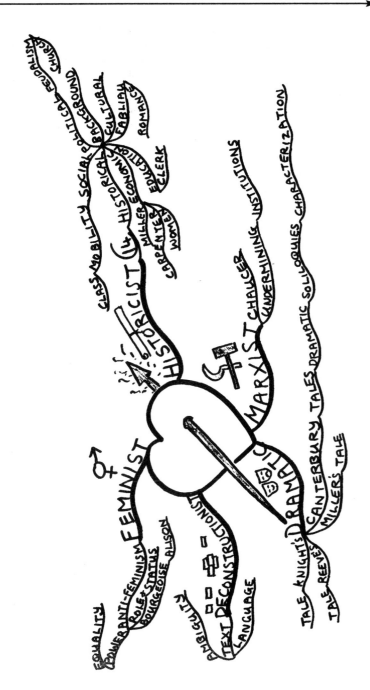

HOW TO GET AN 'A' IN ENGLISH LITERATURE

In all your study, in coursework, and in exams, be aware of the following:

- **Characterization** – the characters and how we know about them (e.g. speech, actions, author description), their relationships, and how they develop.
- **Plot and structure** – story and how it is organized into parts or episodes.
- **Setting and atmosphere** – the changing physical scene and how it reflects the story (e.g. a storm reflecting chaos).
- **Style and language** – the author's choice of words, and literary devices such as imagery, and how these reflect the **mood**.
- **Viewpoint** – how the story is told (e.g. through an imaginary narrator, or in the third person but through the eyes of one character – 'She was furious – how dare he!').
- **Social and historical context** – the author's influences (see 'Context', p. 7).
- **Critical approaches** – different ways in which the text has been, or could be, interpreted.

Develop your ability to:

- Relate **detail** to **broader content, meaning and style**.
- Show understanding of the author's **intentions, technique and meaning** (brief and appropriate comparisons with other works by the same author will gain marks).
- Give **personal response and interpretation**, backed up by **examples** and short **quotations**.
- **Evaluate** the author's achievement (how far does she/he succeed – give reasons).

Make sure you:

- Use **paragraphs** and **sentences** correctly.
- Write in an appropriate **register** – formal but not stilted.
- Use short, appropriate quotations as **evidence** of your understanding.
- Use **literary terms** correctly to explain how an author achieves effects.

THE EXAM ESSAY

Planning

You will probably have about 45 minutes for one essay. It is worth spending 5–10 minutes planning it. An excellent way to do this is in the three stages below.

1 **Mind Map** your ideas, without worrying about their order yet.
2 **Order** the relevant ideas (the ones that really relate to the question) by numbering them in the order in which you will write the essay.
3 **Gather** your evidence and short quotes.

You could remember this as the **MOG** technique.

Writing and checking

Then write the essay, allowing five minutes at the end for checking relevance, spelling, grammar and punctuation.

Remember!

Stick to the question and always **back up** your points with evidence in the form of examples and short quotations. Note: you can use '…' for unimportant words missed out in a quotation.

Model answer and plan

The next (and final) chapter consists of an answer to an exam question on *The Miller's Prologue and Tale*, with the Mind Map and plan used to write it. Don't be put off if you think you couldn't write an essay like this yet. You'll develop your skills if you work at them. Even if you're reading this the night before the exam, you can easily memorize the MOG technique in order to do your personal best.

The model answer and plan are good examples to follow, but don't learn them by heart. It's better to pay close attention to the wording of the question you choose to answer, and allow Mind Mapping to help you to think creatively and structurally.

Before reading the answer, you might like to do a plan of your own to compare with the example. The numbered points, with comments at the end, show why it's a good answer.

M ODEL ANSWER AND ESSAY PLAN

QUESTION

Is *The Miller's Tale* suited to its teller?

PLAN

- The Miller's character and background.
- Reference to Prologue: the predicted tale, opinions of marriage.
- The Tale itself.
- Poetry, style and tone of the Tale.
- The narrator: – the Miller; Chaucer.

ESSAY

The Miller insists on thrusting his tale on the assembled company after the Knight has told his story declaring that he has a tale which not only will 'quite' the Knight's but is also 'noble': 'I kan a noble tale for the nones,/ With which I wol now quite the Knightes tale.' However, it is far from a 'noble' story. In fact the Tale is a racy, ribald narrative which we are told to ignore if we do not approve of it.[1]

The Miller is introduced in the Prologue as a big brute of a man, coarse and forthright. He refuses to be dissuaded from telling his story; indeed we are told that he enjoys telling stories of 'harlotrie', and this Tale is no exception.[2] The minute the Reeve, a carpenter by trade, hears that the proposed Tale involves a carpenter and his wife, he objects violently. This leads the Miller to say why he thinks that it is important not to spy on the sex life of wives, or probe God's secrets. These themes – cuckoldry and the sounding out of celestial secrets – are both repeated in his subsequent tale.[3] John and Nicholas both refer to 'Goddes privetee'; John considers astrological studies are prying into the secrets of the Almighty, and fears that Nicholas might bring divine retribution upon himself and the household. Nicholas swears John to silence by telling him that he is going to divulge 'Cristes conseil'. This is certainly not

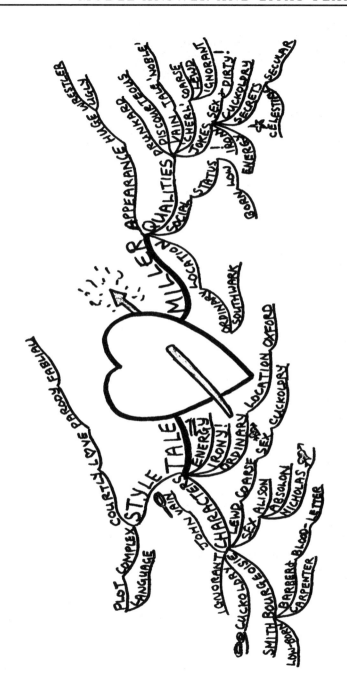

the case (and some may consider Nicholas to be blasphemous in this claim) as all that Nicholas wants to do is to dupe the carpenter so that he can sleep with Alison.

As far as cuckoldry is concerned we might consider that if John had actually pried into Alison's affairs he might not have been cuckolded. Cuckoldry is something the Reeve cannot bear the thought of, and something the Miller would like to believe would not happen to him. In this way, therefore, the Tale is suited to the Miller, as the Tale and Prologue are linked thematically.[4]

The Tale the Miller tells involves people that the Miller would know: a carpenter, a barber and a pretty country girl. They engage in activities of ordinary people: working in the house; collecting wood to use in the carpentry business; hammering metal in a smithy. They also engage in gossip, visiting taverns and love-affairs.[5] They are not part of an idealistic, romantic world of courtly love (indeed the Miller as a character no doubt has absolutely no time for such 'noble' conventions).[6] The characters in the Miller's story inhabit the 'real' world and real places – Oxford and the surrounding areas.[7] The neighbour-hood is recognizable – the carpenter's house with its low window, the smithy over the road and the local church. The geography of John's house is described in detail, down to the cat-hole in the skirting leading to John's room. These are places and house with which the Miller would be familiar, not stately castles, or manors with beautifully tended rose gardens as described in 'The Knight's Tale'.[8]

The Miller himself is coarse and lewd, and is described as a 'cherl'.[9] It is fitting therefore for the Miller to introduce us to similar lewd individuals. The four main characters – John, Alison, Nicholas and Absolon – are all flawed human beings, not noble knights and virtuous maidens. They are, to a greater or lesser extent, vain, selfish and heartless. John, the carpenter, has married a woman much younger than himself, the 18-year-old Alison. He is described as keeping her 'narwe in cage', like a prized possession. When Nicholas grabs her she declares that she fears for her life, 'I woot right wel I nam but deed'.[10] John is also a conceited man who congratulates himself on his lack of education and reveals himself to feel both distaste and awe of Nicholas's learning.

Alison also is a character to whom we are not particularly endeared. In spite of her half-hearted protests she readily agrees to sleep with Nicholas, and shows herself to be coarse, and also heartless towards Absolon. She makes her feelings very clear, calls him a 'Jakke fool', threatens to throw stones at him if he refuses to leave her alone, and then humiliates him with the 'misplaced kiss'. Both the rival lovers, Nicholas and Absolon, are vain and lewd. Nicholas enjoys secret affairs and grabs Alison in what is, in effect, a form of sexual assault. He is also extremely conceited about his learning. Absolon likes to think of himself as a romantic, noble hero, and is effeminate and over-fastidious.[11] All these characters are unlikeable and we watch them with fascination and amusement. The Miller does not charm us either, with his behaviour and attitude. On the whole therefore the individuals we meet in his Tale and the Miller are well-suited![12]

The Tale itself is a tale of seduction, lust and adultery.[13] Included in it are all the other attributes of a bawdy story which might appeal to the Miller: sexual attraction, sexual assault, lovemaking, nakedness and various references to human excretory processes. In fact, what we were promised was a 'cherles' tale, and we are not disappointed. In addition to lewdness there is also comedy in the form of farce: moonings, brandings and tumblings from the ceiling.[14] It is a tale that matches the pace and energy of the Miller, and has about it something of the comic grotesque which is akin to the Miller's own appearance and behaviour.[15] The morals of these people do not offend the Miller; he just presents us with a picture of flawed individuals, puts them in a context of comic farce, and shows them receiving (with the exception of Alison) their various come-uppances.

However, it is not possible to discern the personality of the Miller in his Tale.[16] This is because it is a story which it would be impossible for a drunken Miller to tell in terms of poetry, style and complexity. For example, although the characters use idiomatic language at times, on the whole they do not use language which is 'realistic', that is, exactly as it would have been spoken. Occasionally we are presented with far more colloquial language, such as Gervase's dialogue with Absolon, or Alison's yells from her window. However, none of them would have spoken in iambic pentameter or rhyming couplets – and certainly not a drunken Miller – but the vivacity and humour is enough to suspend our disbelief[17] such is the mastery of Chaucer's poetry. The narrator in the Prologue apologizes for the ensuing Tale, stating that as the Miller was a 'cherl' the tale would be a lewd one. He then goes on to say that:

> I moot reherce
> Hir tales alle, be they bettre or werse,
> Or elles falsen som of my mateere.[18]

In other words the narrator-poet is saying that he has to be true to the characters and the Tales they tell. This is a sophisticated device to ensure that the audience or the reader is prepared to suspend disbelief, thus allowing Chaucer to distance himself from his poem. In this way Chaucer can create a variety of stories covering the whole social spectrum.[19] A man such as the Miller would not have been able to create the wonderful parody of courtly love and its conventions which his Tale presents; neither would he have been likely to come across the fabliau, the genre to which this story belongs.[20] The structure of the tale itself, with shifts of perspective, the absurdly logical twists of plot, the often elegant descriptions and reflections such as 'Lo, which a greet thing is affeccioun!/ Men may dyen of imaginacioun', the references to Cato and astrology – none of these seem suited to the Miller. They seem more to belong to the learned and sophisticated Chaucer. Chaucer had a passion for astrology, like Nicholas, and had written 'Treatise on the Astrolabe'. It is difficult to believe that a man as coarse and uneducated as the Miller would have had a grasp of Latin literature, astrology and astronomy.[21]

To conclude therefore, the Tale itself with its bawdy comedy, and vulgar, ignorant characters, could be seen to be well suited to a character such as the Miller. However, the complexity of the narrative, the structure of the Tale, references to scholarship, and much of the poetic language suggests the presence of a much more sophisticated, learned, and cultured author.[22]

WHAT EARNED THE MARKS

1 Strong opening statement forms basis of essay – shows awareness of *The Miller's Tale* in the context of other Tales.

2 Shows awareness of character.

3 Awareness of thematic links between Prologue and Tale.

4 Good use of evidence.

5 Awareness of characters in Tale supported by evidence from text.

6 Shows awareness of literary genre in context of the quotation.

7 Moves neatly on to next point.

8 Awareness of narrative style and its appropriateness.

9 Recognition of character in context of the question.

10 Apt use of quotation.

11 Good use of evidence.

12 Personal response linked to question demands.

13 Awareness of narrative content in the context of the question demands.

14 Awareness of type of humour – farce.

15 Perceptive comparison of narrative style to Miller's character.

16 Response about extent of Tale's suitability.

17 Awareness of linguistic style – colloquialism; rhyming couplets.

18 Good use of quotation.

19 Comment about authorial voice and intention.

20 Recognition of character and genre – courtly love; fabliaux.

21 Good use of background information and references to text to reinforce argument of essay.

22 Concise conclusion summarizing main argument – response to the extent of agreement with the essay question.

SUGGESTED ALTERNATIVE APPROACH

1 Chaucer's 'meaning' is like Chinese boxes – meaning inside meaning inside meaning. So the answer to the question 'Is *The Miller's Tale* suited to its teller?' depends on the level at which the question is asked.

2 At the obvious level, it is well suited. The Miller is a coarse, low-class person. The Tale is bawdy farce. The Miller is an obvious contrast to the Knight, and also to the Reeve. The Miller pushes himself forward after the Knight has told his Tale with typical vulgar haste. The Miller, we have been told, can butt a door down with his head. He rushes into his Tale as he would rush at a closed door.

3 The Reeve is a much more complex character than the Miller, and yet *The Reeve's tale* is perhaps the most straightforward tale in all *The Canterbury Tales*. (Incidentally, the Knight is not a straightforward gentleman.)

4 As the Miller is someone who rushes at things, knocks doors off their hinges, the plot of his Tale does suit his character: Absolon woos Alison correctly according to the rules of medieval romance – with songs. Nicholas grabs her in the crutch; that is how the Miller would treat a woman. After a while Nicholas does get to sleep with Alison.

5 But there are plenty of images which warn us not to leave the meaning of the Tale at that level. People in real life do not act according to type, and Chaucer knew that very well. Absolon, we hear, sings treble 'he song som time a loud quinible'; but he tries to act Herod on stage, 'Somtime, to shewe his lightnese and maistrie,/ He pleyeth Herodes upon a scaffold hye', and everyone would know that Herod was always played by huge men with big voices – people like the Miller. Then John, the carpenter, thinking Nicholas has gone mad with his astrology, describes how a clerk looking up at the stars fell into a clay-pit:
So ferde another clerk with astromie;/ He walked in the feeldes, for to prye/ Upon the sterres, what ther sholde bifalle/ Til he was in a marle-pit yfalle, when, at the climax of the tale, it is the carpenter himself, who falls.

6 The action of the Tale is not straightforward, and, therefore, does not suit the Miller at all. One day the carpenter goes away to Osney: *And so bifel it on a Saterday, /This*

carpenter was goon til Osenay. Nicholas and Alison are left on their own; they have already made up their minds to sleep together. Why do they not do so immediately? That is what the Miller would have done. Instead Nicholas devises the immensely complicated plan to make the carpenter believe a Noah's Flood is coming. Why waste time on all that? At the beginning of the Tale we hear the carpenter kept Alison *narwe in cage*, but from her behaviour she does not seem to have stayed put in whatever this cage was.

7 What happens at the end of the Tale? Nicholas and Alison shout that the carpenter is mad, and so no one takes any notice of him. As we listen to the telling of the Tale, we see the farcical finalé, and laugh at everyone's situation – the carpenter with his broken arm, being thought mad; Absolon humiliated; Nicholas with his burnt backside. Afterwards, we may wonder 'What happened next?' We then guess that nothing much did happen. There is no indication that Nicholas and Alison lived happy ever after. They have slept together, but only once, and after that night Nicholas will have to spend as much time as possible standing up. It is not a happy love story, but a story of a supposedly educated man who has, for all his education, grabbed sex with the same subtlety as the Miller going through a door by taking it off its hinges. At this level the Tale is very well suited to the Miller.

GLOSSARY OF LITERARY TERMS

alliteration   the repetition, for effect, of consonant sounds at the beginnings of words or syllables.

allusion   the use of literary, cultural and historical references.

assonance   the repetition, for effect, of vowel sounds.

caricature   exaggeration and simplification of character traits.

characterization   the way in which characters are presented.

colloquial   in the language of ordinary conversation.

context   the background of social, historical and literary influences on a work.

dialect   regional form of language varying from the standard in vocabulary and grammar.

diction   choice and arrangement of words.

didactic   intended to instruct; in literary criticism, often used in negative sense.

discursive   presenting a logical argument, step by step.

digression   part of a discourse not on the main subject.

dramatic narrative   story with a lot of dramatic action.

epistolary novel   genre of fiction in which the plot unfolds through letters.

fabliau   short **metrical** tale characterized by vivid, realistic detail and an erotic plot line which was usually comic, coarse, irreverent and cynical.

feminist criticism   critical approach developed in the 1960s, based on assessing the role of gender in texts. A particular issue is the subordination of women in a patriarchal society.

folktale   popular story handed down orally from generation to generation.

free indirect speech   technique blending a character's words and thoughts with narrator's.

genre   the categorizing of artistic works on the basis of form, style, or subject matter; e.g. picaresque novel.

Gothic novel   genre of fiction popular in the eighteenth century, in which eerie and supernatural events take place in sinister settings.

iambic pentameter   verse *metre* with five pairs of syllables in each line, with the stress in each pair placed on the second syllable.

idiom   a characteristic expression of a language or **dialect**.

image   a word picture bringing an idea to life by appealing to the senses.

irony   a style of writing in which one thing is said and another is meant, used for a variety of effects, such as criticism or ridicule.

magical realism   a fiction style which combines mythical elements, bizarre events and a strong sense of cultural tradition, e.g. *Midnight's Children* by Salman Rushdie.

Marxist criticism   critical approach which sees literature in relation to class struggle, and assesses the way texts present social realities.

metaphor   a compressed **simile** describing something as if it were something else.

metre/metrical   rhythm in a line of verse.

narrator   in a novel, a character who tells the story. An *omniscient* narrator has complete knowledge of everything that takes place in the narrative; an *unreliable* narrator is one whose knowledge and judgements are limited and biased.

onomatopoeia   use of words whose sound imitates the thing they describe.

paradox   an apparently contradictory statement which contains some truth; e.g. 'I hear her hair has turned quite gold from grief' (*The Importance of Being Earnest*).

parody   an exaggerated copy (especially of a writer's style) made for humorous effect.

persona   an assumed identity.

personification   an **image** speaking of something abstract, such as love, death or sleep, as if it were a person or a god.

picaresque   type of novel popular in the eighteenth century, featuring the adventures of a wandering rogue; e.g. *Tom Jones* by Henry Fielding.

plot   the story; the events that take place and how they are arranged.

polemical   (of style) making an argument.

reversal turning a theme or convention upside down.

rhetorical   expressed with a view to persuade (often used in negative sense).

romance   tale of chivalry, originally written in verse.

rhyming couplet   a pair of rhyming lines.

satire   literature which humorously exposes and ridicules vice and folly.

simile   an **image** comparing two things similar in some way but different in others, normally using 'like' or 'as'.

soliloquy   an instance of talking to or conversing with oneself, or of uttering one's thoughts aloud without addressing any person (especially in drama).

standard English   the particular form of English, originally based on East Midlands dialect, most often used by educated speakers in formal situations.

stream of consciousness   technique exploring the thought processes and unconscious minds of characters; used by writers such as Virginia Woolf and James Joyce.

structure   the organization of a text, e.g. narrative, plot, repeated images and symbols.

subplot   subsidiary plot coinciding with the main plot, often reflecting aspects of it.

symbol   an object or image which represents another (usually abstract) thing.

syntax   grammatical structure, especially sentence word order.

tone   the mood created by a writer's choice and organization of words, e.g. persuasive.

viewpoint   the way a narrator approaches the material and the audience.

INDEX

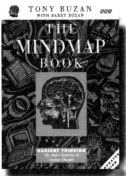